THE ENGLISH REPUBLIC
1649–1660

TE

D0608459

THE ENGLISH REPUBLIC 1649–1660

SECOND EDITION

TOBY BARNARD

Longman
London and New York

Addison Wesley Longman Limited
Edinburgh Gate,
Harlow, Essex CM20 2JE,
United Kingdom
and Associated Companies throughout the world.

*Published in the United States of America
by Addison Wesley Longman Inc., New York*

First published 1982
Tenth impression 1994
Second Edition 1997

ISBN 0 582 080037

British Library Cataloguing in Publication Data

A catalogue record for this book is available from the British Library

Library of Congress Cataloging-in-Publication Data
Barnard, T. C. (Toby Christopher)
    The English Republic, 1649–1660 / Toby Barnard, -- 2nd ed.
        p. cm. -- (Seminar studies in history)
    Includes bibliographical references and index.
    ISBN 0-582-08003-7
    1. Great Britain--Politics and government--1649–1660. I. Title.
II. Series.
DA425.B4 1997
941.06'3--dc21   97-22093
                                                                   CIP

Set by 7 in 10/12 Sabon
Produced through Longman Malaysia, PP

CONTENTS

An introduction to the series   vii
Note on referencing system   viii

PART ONE; THE BACKGROUND   1

1   ENGLAND IN 1649   1
2   THE ARMY AND OLIVER CROMWELL   5

PART TWO: DESCRIPTIVE ANALYSIS   8

3   THE RULE OF THE RUMP PARLIAMENT 1649–1653   8

    The Rump established   8
    Ireland and Scotland   14
    The dissolution of the Rump   17

4   THE FIRST PHASE OF GODLY RULE:
    THE BAREBONES PARLIAMENT OF 1653   24

    Godly rule   24
    The calling of the Barebones Parliament   27
    Parliament dissolved   30

5   THE FIRST PHASE OF HEALING AND SETTLING:
    THE PROTECTORATE   35

    The Instrument of Government   35
    The first months of the Protectorate   38
    The first Protectorate Parliament   43
    Plots and royalist insurrection   47

6   THE SECOND PHASE OF GODLY RULE:
    THE MAJOR-GENERALS 1655–1656   50

    The institution of the major-generals   50
    The major-generals at work   54

7   THE SECOND PHASE OF HEALING AND SETTLING:
    THE LORD PROTECTOR 1656–1658   57

    The end of the major-generals   57
    Kingship   59
    The last months of Cromwell   63

8   EPILOGUE: TOWARDS THE RESTORATION OF CHARLES II   67

    PART THREE: ASSESSMENT   70
9   THE IMPACT OF THE REGIME   70

    PART FOUR: DOCUMENTS   80
    Glossary   94
    Bibliography   97
    Index   106
    Related Titles   111

AN INTRODUCTION TO THE SERIES

Such is the pace of historical enquiry in the modern world that there is an ever-widening gap between the specialist article or monograph, incorporating the results of current research, and general surveys, which inevitably become out of date. *Seminar Studies in History* are designed to bridge this gap. The series was founded by Patrick Richardson in 1966 and his aim was to cover major themes in British, European and World history. Between 1980 and 1996 Roger Lockyer continued his work, before handing the editorship over to Clive Emsley and Gordon Martel. Clive Emsley is Professor of History at the Open University, while Gordon Martel is Professor of International History at the University of Northern British Columbia, Canada and Senior Research Fellow at De Montfort University.

All the books are written by experts in their field who are not only familiar with the latest research but have often contributed to it. They are frequently revised, in order to take account of new information and interpretations. They provide a selection of documents to illustrate major themes and provoke discussion, and also a guide to further reading. The aim of *Seminar Studies* is to clarify complex issues without over-simplifying them, and to stimulate readers into deepening their knowledge and understanding of major themes and topics.

NOTE ON REFERENCING SYSTEM

Readers should note that numbers in square brackets [5] refer them to the corresponding entry in the Bibliography at the end of the book (specific page numbers are given in italics). A number in square brackets preceded by *Doc.* [*Doc.* 5] refers readers to the corresponding item in the Documents section which follows the main text. Words which are defined in the Glossary are asterisked on their first occurrence in the book.

PART ONE: THE BACKGROUND

1 ENGLAND IN 1649

By 1649 an uneasy peace had settled over England after seven years of intermittent civil wars. Only a minority of zealots had wanted war when it broke out in August 1642; when it ended in 1646 even fewer approved it. The political instability of the 1650s arose largely from varied reactions to the war years. By way of introduction we must describe how the more serious differences originated.

When the Long Parliament assembled in November 1640 its members were virtually united in condemning the royal policies of the preceding decade. Parliament legislated to prevent those policies being repeated. It guaranteed regular meetings for itself and punished the authors of recent acts. Parliament divided when veteran critics of the king, led by Lord Bedford and John Pym, revealed their programme. They asked the king for the great offices of state, so that they might simultaneously profit and protect the nation from the king's efforts to erect an absolutism on the continental model. Charles I angrily refused to forfeit his traditional prerogative to choose his own ministers. By requesting office Pym antagonised many who had happily supported him so long as he attacked only the innovations of the 1630s. When, in 1641, the backwoodsmen in parliament discovered that decentralised and cheap government, exercised mainly by the justices of the peace,* was not Pym's prime aim and that instead he wished parliament to pay more towards the expenses of government in return for an end to the king's right to select his ministers and army commanders, many detached themselves from Pym and turned neutral or royalist. The movement in Charles I's favour was accelerated by the religious radicalism, apparently connived at by Pym, which first drove the bishops from the House of Lords and then threatened them with abolition.

The divisions within parliament, between a minority with national priorities and anxious to capture government and a traditionalist majority whose horizons were bounded either by their estates, by their parishes or by their shires, deepened once civil war broke out.

Local efforts to avert conflict had failed. Experience of warfare soon confirmed the gloomy prognostications and swelled the numbers of those who urged an immediate cessation to the fighting. Unruly soldiers rampaged through the countryside, wasting property and intimidating civilians; taxes multiplied until an unheard of proportion of national wealth drained away to Westminster; the operations of the law courts were temporarily suspended; familiar institutions of county and town government, notably the commission of the peace,* were superseded by new county committees intended to be more subservient to the central government; and even the customary local hierarchies were endangered as men from outside the usual circle of country rulers took command of the forces and the shire administrations. Parliament by 1645 ruled more tightly, arbitrarily and expensively than Charles I had ever done [84, 86, 87].

Parliament's innovations won it the war, but the victory cost parliament the scant popularity it had enjoyed in 1642. With the war finished it was expected that parliament would settle with the king. Any treaty would surely see parliament shed its recently assumed powers, dismantle the novel institutions in the localities, and disband its expensive armies. When no treaty was signed and the costly novelties continued, parliament was blamed. Its members and their friends in the provinces were suspected of prolonging the emergency for their own profit.

Nationwide impatience turned to anger as a succession of bad harvests increased food prices and unemployment worsened. A majority of MPs wanted to conclude a treaty, but could not. Peace-making was complicated by the attitude of a part of the army, linked with a minority of MPs and well-organised radicals in London and other towns. Some soldiers, seeing themselves as the architects of parliament's success, expected to shape the coming settlement. They proposed to reduce the king's power to choose ministers and army officers, and insisted on a measure of religious freedom. They also asked that the ordinary soldiers should be compensated for their considerable sacrifices. By 1647 a section of parliament's forces was prepared to stop any settlement which did not satisfy it [79, 129].

Parliament was also hampered by the king, who saw neither the necessity nor the propriety of acceding to its terms. Charles calculated, realistically enough, that his enemies – parliament, its allies in Scotland and its armies – would soon fall out among themselves. Then he would be able to detach at least one element in the parliamentary coalition. Furthermore he expected help, either from his English subjects, wearied by parliament's oppressions, or from Scotland,

Ireland or the Continent. By 1648 dislike of parliamentarian rule was expressed in armed risings [50, 79]. Royalists too easily mistook this disillusionment with parliament for enthusiasm for Charles I. Those who attempted to turn the insurrections to the king's advantage saw the revolts quickly collapse. However, Charles had succeeded in engaging the aid of some Scots, who in June 1648 invaded England. The events of 1648 – the Second Civil War – reminded parliament of its feeble hold over the country. Most MPs responded by redoubling their efforts to agree with Charles I, as the only method to recover popularity. The new war affected the soldiery and their friends very differently. The seemingly invincible army regarded itself as an instrument chosen by God to refashion England. The king, clearly the author of the recent war, having invited in the Scots, was now described in the army as 'that man of blood' who had to be called to account [144 *p. 54*].

By the autumn of 1648 parliament and its forces were seriously at odds. The former was prepared to waive many of its earlier demands in order to reach an agreement with the king, and proposed that he return to London, where a popular reaction in his favour was likely. The army commanders, abetted by MPs like Henry Marten and Edmund Ludlow, acted to prevent parliament taking steps which might well culminate in Charles I's unconditional restoration. On 3 December 1648 Colonel Pride forcibly prevented about 100 MPs reputed to favour concessions to the king from sitting in the Commons. The Long Parliament, first elected in 1640, now had fewer than 200 active members. Nevertheless it still claimed to represent the entire nation of five million [115].

Pride's Purge was merely the first act in a programme which dangerously isolated the purged or 'Rump' Parliament and the army from the population. The king's duplicity and obstinacy made him too untrustworthy to be restored to his old position. In January 1649 the Rump authorised an entirely novel High Court of Justice to try him for high treason. The king showed his contempt for the newly minted doctrines of treason by refusing to acknowledge the authority of the court. The latter hurriedly declared him guilty. On 30 January 1649, outside the new Banqueting House in Whitehall, Charles I was beheaded [124].

Some had toyed with the idea of substituting another Stuart for the stubborn Charles I, but none could be found to do parliament's bidding. Monarchy had to be replaced, but the Rump were ill-prepared. After some fumbling, in March the Rump abolished monarchy in England, and then, after more delay, declared England 'a Commonwealth and Free State' on 19 May 1649. Reluctantly the Rump had made a revolution. The changes were half-hearted impro- visations. Ideological republicans were rare in England. Some among the educated had visited or read of the continental republics of Holland and Venice; the godly knew that Scripture commended republics [51, 107, 193]. Only the unexpected intransigence of the defeated Charles I had forced his opponents into revolution and republicanism as the way out of the political impasse. But killing the king, the most unpopular of a series of unpopular acts, created fresh problems. The revolutionaries could settle and control the country only if they found a popular alternative to monarchy. For the mom- ent the army deterred malcontents from working actively against the Rump and for the Stuarts' restoration. The Rump's dependence on the army was dangerous, and needed to be replaced with a wider following. As we shall see, the Rump strove in vain to enlarge its support, and ended by antagonising the soldiery.

2 THE ARMY AND OLIVER CROMWELL

The army, called into being by parliament, in turn created the Rump and then partnered it in revolution. Before tracing the collapse of the uncomfortable alliance, let us consider the army and its commanders before 1649.

No army in the 1640s, whether the king's or parliament's, was liked by civilians. In the early stages of the First Civil War parliament's forces were as unruly as, and more incompetent than, the royalist regiments. Most were recruited and fought in a small area, and were commanded by local landowners. Conditions of service were poor, with irregular pay and rampant disease, so that many soldiers deserted. As supplies slowly improved and as officers were promoted on their merits, discipline tightened. In 1645, after a violent political battle, timid aristocratic commanders were retired and the regional armies were refashioned, part of them as the New Model Army. The latter, commanded by Thomas Fairfax and its cavalry led by Oliver Cromwell, was favoured with regular supplies and pay by parliament. The New Model's reputation was made by its victory over the King at Naseby. Once heroic exploits gave way in 1646 to tedious garrison duties, the soldiers incurred the hatred of townspeople. Some soldiers, encouraged by their officers and radical preachers, reflected on their own plight, on the straits of the civilians from whose ranks they had recently been plucked and into which they would soon return, and on the kingdom's future. Naturally the soldiers worried about their pay, much of which was owed by parliament; who would command and where they would be sent next; how the widows and orphans of their slain comrades could be helped, and what they themselves would do when demobilised. By 1647 these soldiers feared parliament, for it intended to regain popularity by sending some of them to reconquer Ireland and by disbanding the remainder. MPs hoped by these means simultaneously to reduce taxes and to free themselves from the soldiers' meddling [75, 85, 87, 129].

These plans enraged many soldiers, some of whom had followed attentively recent political and religious controversies. The soldiery vowed to remain united until parliament satisfied their material worries. In published apologias the soldiers explained why they had disobeyed parliament's orders. Furthermore, they impugned the present parliament, which had treated them so badly, as unrepresentative of the nation and as dominated by corrupt and self-interested men. The soldiers argued that as free-born Englishmen they had the right to air their complaints and to promote the interests of the entire population in the new settlement. The officers had been assisted in their deliberations by elected agents from the rank-and-file, the Agitators. As the army criticised parliament and stated its desires, it was far from united. Fairfax and Cromwell, although sympathetic to their men's professional grievances, believed that politics should be left to parliament. By August 1647, it was clear that parliament was controlled by members careless of the army's problems and of the nation's safety, and Fairfax and Cromwell reluctantly supported the army marching on London and expelling from parliament those who were too friendly to Charles [129].

Once parliament had been remodelled, Cromwell hoped that it could be left to treat with the king. But a small knot of radicals, some soldiers and some civilians from London, had acquired a taste for politics. They now expected to shape the coming settlement, and produced a clumsy compendium of political, social and religious reforms which were to be included. The Levellers' proposals went beyond the familiar wish to restrict the king's powers, to replace the present parliament and to alter the structure of the state Church, and suggested that future parliaments, if they were to avoid the weaknesses of the Long Parliament, should be elected on a different franchise and for redistributed constituencies, and that the maximum as well as minimum life should be stipulated. These schemers also considered how to pay the clergy more equitably, how to make the law courts cheaper and easier to use, how to provide work and share profitable trade, how to relieve the poor and sick more efficiently, and how to help those who in increasing numbers had fallen into debt during the war [28, 29, 38, 47, 57, 79].

Cromwell allowed the divisive debate until he needed to use the army. Then he summarily silenced the few Levellers and returned wholeheartedly to his tactic of working through parliament to achieve a satisfactory settlement. Cromwell's policy changed on the outbreak of the Second Civil War. He and Fairfax were fully stretched in suppressing a dangerous insurrection clearly engineered by the king.

Parliament at the same time had resumed its talks with Charles, and dropped some of the conditions on which it had earlier insisted. Faced with the prospect of a treaty which would restore, on too generous terms, a monarch now deeply distrusted, Cromwell and Fairfax were prepared to let the army block the unacceptable settlement. Cromwell himself could not completely overcome his repugnance at the soldiers usurping the MPs' role, and left the practical arrangements to others. However, once parliament had been purged, Cromwell worked hard to enlist support for the sickly Rump. At the same time he explored ways by which Charles I might be retained as king [115]. None could be found, and Cromwell accepted the inevitability of Charles's trial and execution. Cromwell, like many Rumpers, became a reluctant revolutionary. He had been converted, largely through the king's own deviousness, to the view that Charles I was too dangerous to be spared. Yet Cromwell was still attached to traditional institutions. He had wanted to retain the monarchy and had pleaded for the retention of the House of Lords. When those institutions were swept away, Cromwell bowed to the changes as the working out of divine providence. Henceforward he would try other forms of government so long as they satisfied two needs. One was to stabilise the exhausted and divided country by devising a government which would be solidly supported in the provinces; the other was to please the victors by forwarding godly reformation. Soon enough Cromwell discovered that few shared both objectives and that his twin aims of a stable and godly nation were incompatible.

PART TWO: DESCRIPTIVE ANALYSIS

3 THE RULE OF THE RUMP PARLIAMENT 1649-1653

THE RUMP ESTABLISHED

The revolution which had killed the king, abolished the monarchy and substituted a Commonwealth, had been made by a small group of MPs and some army officers. The survival of the unloved new régime was from the start uncertain. The army had to shield the Commonwealth against its enemies: plotters in England and possible invaders on behalf of Charles Stuart, Charles I's eldest son, from Scotland, Ireland or the continent. Between 1649 and 1653 the size of the army increased from 47,000 to 60,000 men, and the tax burden grew proportionately. Notwithstanding the Rumpers' preferences, the régime inevitably depended on the soldiers for its life. But even the large army could not guarantee success for the revolution. It might defeat challengers but it could not engender support in London or the provinces.

The Commonwealth was weak because few had actively wanted it and because even those who had created it, the Rumpers and the officers, expected different results from it. The soldiers thought they had acquired a parliament which would speedily draft a new constitution and then transfer power to a fresh parliament. The Rump, while finalising the details of this novel system, was expected to start the long-delayed reform of society and the Church, and to allay the soldiers' professional grievances. But those who looked for reform, the soldiers, the Levellers and the members of the autonomous religious congregations, disagreed about the nature and even the necessity of the proposed changes.

The Levellers tended to concentrate on secular matters, such as reducing taxes, curbing the arbitrary powers assumed by parliament and bestowed promiscuously on its local agents, breaking the hurtful monopoly over lucrative trade enjoyed by the great London companies, and protecting agricultural tenants against their landlords. The Levellers shared with the army a wish to curtail the might of parliament. Years lived under the Long Parliament had taught even its former supporters that it was not the expected protector of men's liberties. The Levellers argued that the people were sovereign, and though the people might delegate power to a parliament, the latter must be made more accountable and more sensitive to the people's wishes. To this end it was proposed to redistribute parliamentary seats, giving more to the counties where the bulk of the population lived and where voters were freer to express their preferences, and fewer to the towns, which could more easily be controlled by the wealthy and powerful. It was also recommended that the electorate be increased, though reformers differed on whether to use rate or tax paying or mere residence as the qualification [31, 47, 78].

In contrast, most sectaries* thought chiefly of building the New Jerusalem. To achieve that, the gospel must first be purified and then spread more thoroughly, especially in the neglected and remote north and Wales. Restraints which had stopped godly men from preaching and which inhibited the free growth of congregations must be removed. Even secular institutions, like parliament and the law courts, had to be brought into conformity with the word of God [65, 80, 81, 113].

Radicals and sectaries deluged the Rump with contradictory proposals. Mistakenly the Rump ignored their requests. Although soldiers and radicals disagreed about the exact form of changes, most insisted that changes must come. Buoyed up by a remarkable series of victories, and emboldened by the unthinkable that had been accomplished, the toppling of a monarch, they wished to complete their revolution. Only when pressed by the army did the Rump attend to reform – in the summer of 1649, the winter of 1649–50, and the autumns of 1650 and 1651. Until 1652 these occasional flurries of activity, inspired usually by Cromwell, satisfied the busy soldiers. Then the officers scrutinised the Rump's record and saw how poor it was. A few MPs, like the libertine and committed republican Henry Marten, shared the soldiers' and radicals' priorities [Williams in 96, 130]. Most Rumpers, however, regarded their chief work as governing the country, a full-time task. The Rumpers saw no urgency about transferring their power to a successor. The MPs, some of whom had sat continuously at Westminster since 1640, had become too accustomed to power to relinquish it willingly. This wish to cling to their positions was not, as the army contended, entirely self-interested. MPs argued convincingly that the country was still too unsettled to hold new elections, which would only return royalists. The Rumpers' reluctance to retire into the provincial obscurity from which they had come, led many historians to label them as corrupt profiteers. That hostile assessment of the Rump, fostered by those who removed it in 1653, has been challenged [130]. The Rump can be defended on the grounds that many of the expectations of what it might do were unrealistic, and that its members adequately performed those humdrum but essential tasks which they set themselves. As an assembly, the Rump was neither better nor worse than other seventeenth-century parliaments. Certainly the older view that depicted the Rumpers as fervent revolutionaries intent on overturning the familiar landmarks in Church and state has been convincingly refuted. Those in the Rump who had schemed to be rid of the king were a minority – no more than seventy. Those already committed to republicanism in 1649 were a small handful. The majority of Rumpers sat on in parliament because thereby they might curb revolutionary excesses, bring government back into more traditional channels and, at the same time, forward their own and their constituents' interests.

Yet the Rumpers differed in some vital ways from the members of other seventeenth-century parliaments. Their powers, their history and their present tasks all made them unique. Never before had parliament acted as executive as well as legislature and governed the realm. Many of the MPs had successfully run a war against the king, and in doing so had mastered complex administrative and financial procedures. For almost nine years they had dwelt in London. More recently they had authorised the trial and execution of their sovereign, and, albeit reluctantly, invented the Commonwealth. In 1649 the MPs confronted unique problems: how to govern a restless state, to create provincial enthusiasm and to frustrate possible invasions. The Rumpers were also expected to restore harmony and prosperity to the country, and to inaugurate expensive and controversial reforms.

The Rump, like all earlier parliaments, contained drones and the negligent, but the parochial mentality of the backwoodsman, ever critical and uncomprehending of the London government, which had prevailed in earlier assemblies and which would reappear after 1654, was much less pronounced. A majority, for the first time in a parliament, was willing to rule the country, raise taxes, deploy armies and treat with foreign powers. The political expertise and experience of the Rump would be remembered, and help to explain the fond memory which politicians had of the Rump as the decade passed. Yet the very professionalism of the Rumpers separated them from the provincial opinions which they were meant to represent. As a result, the Rump failed to focus on itself the enthusiasm and loyalty which was traditionally attached to the institution of parliament. When the Rump was dissolved, few publicly lamented its passing.

Ardent republicans (admittedly a small group) were dissatisfied because the timid creation of the Commonwealth had not been accompanied by other fundamental institutional changes. They complained that England could easily be made a monarchy again, and suspected that this had been the Rumpers' intention [*Doc. 3*]. It is true that many, inside and outside parliament, hankered after monarchy as the form of government best suited to England. This feeling grew as constitutional experiments failed to please the country [*Doc. 2*]. The Rump, uninterested in ideological changes, concentrated on making basic government function.

The parliament transferred some of its executive work to a Council of State. Although this Council was empowered to deploy the army and navy, to settle diplomatic and commercial questions, and, rather vaguely, to advise on the good of the Commonwealth, it lacked independence from the Rump. It tended to despatch the business referred to it by parliament, with the latter still taking the important decisions. Furthermore its membership, elected annually, was determined by, and consisted for the most part of, Rumpers. The Council was an enlarged version of the parliamentary committees which had transacted business for the Long Parliament in the 1640s. It also realised a scheme, mooted by Pym and most recently included in the army manifestoes of 1647 and 1648, for making the king's Privy Council accountable to parliament. Charles I had haughtily resisted these changes. But now many of the executive and advisory tasks previously performed by the Privy Council were given to this new council subservient to parliament.

The identity of the councillors (about forty in all) changed considerably each year as the Rumpers removed political opponents or the lazy. Although unwieldy in size, the Council of State directed national affairs competently enough. Many of its members had, after all, accumulated useful administrative experience in the 1640s, either on parliament's committees, or commanding armies, and governing the counties. Moreover, the councillors were assisted by a skilled secretariat which had acquired expertise in the 1640s [33, 130].

The concentration of power in the hands of MPs and councillors of state, coupled with their apparent indifference to reform, led quickly to publicly expressed disappointment. Some soldiers, the Levellers and the sectaries maintained that they had been cheated, and that a new tyranny had been substituted for the old [28, 78]. The hostile

Levellers, previously strong in London and influential in the army, might seriously endanger the new régime. Their bitterness arose from the alliance with the army grandees, into which Ireton had cajoled them in the autumn of 1648. Ireton, a close comrade and more recently the son-in-law of Cromwell, had needed to confront the Long Parliament with a united movement, and had secured Leveller participation by holding out the hope that, once the Long Parliament had been remodelled, the Leveller programme would be implemented. But when the Levellers submitted their proposals to the Rump in January 1649 they were ignored. Neither Cromwell nor Ireton would compel the Rump to debate, let alone adopt, the radical scheme. The Levellers rounded on Cromwell and Ireton, who had tricked them, and condemned the Rump as no better than 'a mock Parliament and a mock power' which lacked popular approval [38, 57, 78]. In March 1649 the Levellers prepared to attack the Rump and the army commanders, as they had earlier lambasted the Long Parliament, and with the same weapons: savage lampoons, pithy tracts and large demonstrations in London. Cromwell, now that he, and the state which he had helped to establish, were to be the victims, acted severely. The civil authorities quelled the London disorders, while Cromwell scotched mutinies in the forces.

The ease with which the Levellers were suppressed in 1649 is surprising, and raises the question why the radicals seemed so much weaker in 1649 than they had been in 1647 and 1648. Part of the answer was the change in Cromwell's and Ireton's attitude, from indulgence to hostility. The Levellers' following in the army had probably diminished as some of the men's arrears were paid and as the number of sympathetic officers was reduced. Then too, part of the Levellers' support had been volatile and ephemeral, born of the economic distress which had engulfed the country after 1646. By 1649 harvests were better, though prices did not drop much until 1650. It may also be that some of the Levellers' earlier strength had been illusory. It had always been a heterogeneous movement, thriving among the sectaries and small tradespeople of London. In 1646 the Levellers, faced with an increasingly repressive parliament, with worsening trade and with the injustices of their superiors, had questioned conventional authority. Skilled propagandists had lifted the onslaught on specific oppressions onto a higher plane, formulating ideas of rights once enjoyed but later lost, of natural rights which could never be alienated, of the equality of men and of the sovereignty of the people. The leaders, notably John Lilburne, cleverly seized the opportunities offered by the numerous printing presses in London, by the congregations, livery companies and Common Council of the city through which men could quickly be contacted and organised for action, and by the sheer size of London's population (probably near half a million). When the Levellers defined their programme more precisely, the movement splintered. Nor could the weapons with which they had previously goaded the authorities dislodge a régime determined to survive. No matter how barbed the invective, how witty and apposite the pamphlets or how large the throngs of unarmed civilians, they could not defeat the ruthless Cromwell and the Rump [47, 78, 139, 140].

Many radical critics of the Rump deserted the faltering Leveller movement after the summer of 1649. Some went underground for a time, to resurface later when the Rump looked more vulnerable. A few retreated into local activity. Best-known in that category were the Diggers, who attempted on a Surrey hill to found a community which would show how men could live amicably without private property. The experiment alarmed the conventional, and the Diggers were forcibly dispersed [27, 65]. Other radicals willingly worked for the new régime. The Commonwealth might not have progressed far towards an ideal society, but it was a start. It had already demolished the corrupt institutions of monarchy, House of Lords and bishops. The Rump, short of local assistants, often entrusted power to those who came forward to serve it without inquiring too minutely into their past behaviour or present opinions. In some counties the Rump allowed a dangerous concentration of power to an individual radical and his henchmen. John Pyne in Somerset, Herbert Morley in Sussex, Michael Livesey in Kent, Robert Bennet in Cornwall and Thomas Birch in Lancashire were examples of this [31, 50, 55, 115]. These radical county bosses, being loosely supervised from Westminster, started controversial reforms which the Rump itself was reluctant to tackle. As a result local agents did in the Rump's name what that body would never have approved, and in so doing ensured that the Rump incurred the opprobrium and estranged provincial opinion. In the capital radicals eschewed futile demonstrations and infiltrated the city government until they dominated the Common Council of the corporation.

Cromwell, insistent that the nascent republic should survive, helped the Rump to master domestic enemies. There remained a danger of royalist intrigue. The execution of Charles I had horrified many who had had little sympathy for the king while he lived. A skilfully propagated cult of the royal martyr strengthened royalism. Nevertheless, public manifestations of royalism were rare. Those who had fought for Charles I had either followed his son into exile or were too preoccupied with raising money to pay off fines and repossess their estates to risk their property in new fighting. Royalist sympathisers were deterred from foolhardy behaviour by the fate of those who had risen in the Second Civil War. The antics of their new king, Charles II, made royalists even less inclined to rise. He seemed willing to abandon episcopacy in order to secure Presbyterian* help. Worse still, he was prepared to abase himself before the Scots Presbyterians and to sacrifice much that his father had fought for if, in return, the Scots helped him to regain his throne. A king restored by Scots and Presbyterians was not to the taste of most English royalists, and so they stood aloof.

IRELAND AND SCOTLAND

By the summer of 1649 England had submitted reluctantly to the Rump's rule. Enthusiasm might be negligible, but the lack of serious open dissent was the more significant fact. Elsewhere dangers loomed. A wave of horror had rippled through Europe following Charles I's judicial murder, but the shock was not translated into action against England. Indeed France and Spain, locked in a seemingly endless contest, would soon be courting the revolutionary régime for extra help.

The greatest dangers to the Rump were nearer home, in Ireland and Scotland. England's hold over Ireland, never firm, had been loosened in 1641. As rebellion engulfed Ireland in the 1640s, Charles I played the dangerous game of seeking soldiers from the Catholic insurgents in return for political and religious concessions. These negotiations, when prematurely revealed, had ruined the king's reputation without bringing him useful aid. When the English Civil War ended, parliament sought to re-establish its hold over Ireland. However, the forces it sent were too few, and by 1649 faced a new and more formidable alliance of Irish Catholics and Protestants. The alliance was based on the belief of each group that its interests would be better protected by Charles Stuart than by an English parliament, traditionally anti-Catholic and hostile to Ireland. The alliance, formed too late to save Charles I from the scaffold, might well assist Charles II.

The Rump insisted that the Irish royalists be dislodged. The prospect of soldiering in Ireland had been one cause of the army's restlessness in 1647, and again played a part in the mutinous stirrings of 1649. By 1649 Cromwell agreed with the Rump that the new English Commonwealth would be safe only when the Irish had been subjugated. He took command of an expeditionary force stipulating that it should be sufficient for the task (more than 30,000 men were shipped across the Irish Sea) and properly supplied.

Shortly before Cromwell landed in August 1649 his opponents had been heavily defeated near Dublin and the incongruous alliance of Catholics and Protestants was disintegrating. Nevertheless, he feared a protracted campaign which would waste his army, bankrupt the republic and distract him from other military tasks. Accordingly he dealt swiftly and savagely with the resistance. The inhabitants of Drogheda and Wexford, after refusing to capitulate, were butchered. Cromwell's relish of the carnage, expressed in letters to parliament, [1, ii *pp. 124–8, 140–3*] was approved by his contemporaries and has been condemned by posterity as his most odious characteristic. Cromwell, in massacring these unfortunates, acted to shorten the war. Two other motives influenced his behaviour. The garrisons contained English as well as Irish royalists, and as such were regarded by Cromwell as the last redoubts of that unholy combination called into existence by Charles I in 1648. Everywhere the authors of the Second Civil War had been punished, and Ireland was to be no exception. In addition Cromwell's, and many of his soldiers', outlook on Ireland had been formed by the lurid accounts of the massacres of Protestants which had begun the long war in 1641. Most English and Scottish Protestants believed passionately that they had a God-given duty to avenge the massacres, and it was that task which Cromwell performed with such zest [77, 133, 139, 140].

Cromwell's progress in Ireland was checked; pockets of resistance survived until 1652. However, after nine months, Cromwell re-established nominal English authority over much of Ireland, and ended royalist hopes of using it as a base. The task of making the nominal English authority effective, never easy in Ireland, was immensely complicated by the revolution in England. The Protestants in Ireland, normally the bedrock of government, generally opposed the recent changes in England. In the end, however, most Irish Protestants grudgingly accepted the authority of the Commonwealth and its extension into Ireland because it meant rule by Protestants and Englishmen rather than by Catholics and Irish [134].

Cromwell as commander had reconquered the island. As Lord-Lieutenant he was authorised to recreate a rudimentary administration. With the limited means available he did so, and at the same time used Ireland to show how the law and Church in England might be reformed. The modest reforms accomplished in Ireland, where few men of substance had to be humoured and where no parliament procrastinated, made Cromwell and his associates more critical of the Rump's failure to transform England [*Doc. 4*].

In May 1650 the menace from Scotland necessitated Cromwell's recall from Ireland. The affection of the Scots for the Stuarts (who were the Scots' own dynasty) had not been entirely extinguished in the 1640s. Some Scots had helped Charles I, most recently and disastrously in 1648. Loyalty was strengthened and traditional anti-English feeling was rekindled when the English murdered the King of the Scots. Also, by 1649, many Scots were chafing against the tyrannical rule of the Covenanters,* led by Argyll, to which they had been subjected for the past decade. The Covenanters' alliance with the Long Parliament in 1643 was now described as a miscalculation, for Scotland had gained little in return for its costly contributions. A growing group contended that Scotland would do better to assist the king against the English parliament. Such a policy seemed yet more alluring when the malleable Charles II, desperate for aid, succeeded his father. Charles II quickly agreed to humiliating terms, as a result of which he was brought to Scotland and crowned King of the Scots [39, 71].

Charles II's alliance with the Scots threatened the Rump. The Scots, for their own security, wished to export their distinctive brand of Presbyterianism south of the border. Charles II expected his Scots allies to recapture his English inheritance for him. A fresh Scots invasion of England seemed imminent by the summer of 1650. Cromwell, backed by the Rump, preferred to strike first. Fairfax, disenchanted with the revolution and the repudiation of earlier undertakings, refused to command and was replaced by Cromwell. Cromwell, now Commander-in-Chief, entered Scotland and defeated the Scots at Dunbar on 3 September 1650, arguably his most spectacular victory [*Doc. 1*]. He had contained but not eliminated the danger. Lacking enough troops and with poor lines of supply, he dared not press further into Scotland.

Dunbar demoralised the already factious Scots. Argyll and the stricter Presbyterian clergy had always doubted the value of aligning behind the king, and questioned Charles's sincerity in taking the covenant and promising to protect Presbyterianism. An influential section of the Scottish clergy interpreted Dunbar as a sign of divine disfavour and refused henceforward to assist Charles II. The king, beset by jarring Scottish factions, wished only to break out of Scotland and dash for the heart of England. The rigid clergy prevented the king from mobilising all his potential supporters in Scotland for this plan, and few Englishmen joined him as he marched through England with 12,000 Scots. Cromwell, with a larger army, pursued him closely, pinned him at Worcester and there trounced him on 3 September 1651. The royalist threat to the Commonwealth was ended. Charles slipped into exile. Royalism itself survived, but as a private, almost quietistic faith to be cherished in secluded country manors and Anglican clergymen's studies.

Scotland's association with the defeated Charles II exposed the country to reprisals. The Rump annexed and subordinated Scotland to England. Its independent institutions, such as the Edinburgh Parliament, the executive Committee of Estates and the General Assembly of the Church, were suppressed. Land tenure and the law courts were remodelled on English principles. It was hoped that social and institutional reform would gradually wean the Scots away from their misguided devotion to the Stuarts. Until those policies started to work, the Scots were to be closely supervised by an English army of occupation, for which they would pay through punitive taxation [39, 49].

THE DISSOLUTION OF THE RUMP

After Cromwell's victory at Worcester the soldiery replaced the royalists as the main threat to the Rump's survival. Worcester, the latest in an apparently unbreakable sequence, was for Cromwell the 'crowning mercy' and confirmed that he and his soldiers had been chosen by God to turn England into a godly Commonwealth. After the victory Cromwell and his men, now at leisure, reflected on the Rump's poor progress. At first Cromwell restrained his men, telling them that parliament would attend to reform, but by 1653 he no longer believed his own assurances and gave way to the soldiers' calls for action.

The Rump had not idled away all its time. The laws relating to debtors had been eased. The poor need no longer languish in jail, their families beggared, while rich men evaded their debts. Legal proceedings would be written in a normal hand rather than in a script which only the trained could decipher. The Elizabethan statute requiring weekly attendance at the parish church was repealed. Enquiries were started to make better use of the endowments of the state Church. Large and unwieldy parishes would be divided, and small or poor ones would be united. It was also aimed to pay all incumbents at least £100 annually. The special needs of the north, Wales and Ireland were catered for by Acts to assist the propagation of the gospel in those regions. The Rump's achievements were not derisory, especially when it was simultaneously struggling to survive and to raise money.

Blair Worden commented that 'finance was the unsolved problem which overshadowed Rump politics from beginning to end' [130 *p. 217*]. The Commonwealth at first benefited from enormous windfalls, such as the extensive lands confiscated from the bishops and cathedral deans and chapters (all of which had been abolished) and from the royal family and a group of about 780 prominent royalists. Many of these assets were quickly bespoken, by soldiers whose arrears had somehow to be paid and by those who had lent money to parliament in the 1640s. Unfortunately the Rump treated its wealthy creditors too shabbily for these assets to generate substantial new loans. Furthermore, the land market was suddenly glutted by the vast acreages for sale, and in consequence the state realised only a fraction of the value of the confiscated lands when they were sold.

The Commonwealth might have made more friends, had it economised. But taxes, far from being cut, were increased, first to pay for the Irish and Scottish expeditions, and then after 1652, to finance a war against the Dutch. The Rump was obliged to continue the assessment and the excise, which Pym had introduced as temporary devices. The régime failed to unlock the coffers of the London merchants. This failure – surprising when relations between some Rumpers and the City were close and when merchants appeared to influence policy – testified to the poor way in which the Long Parliament had treated creditors and to a lack of confidence in the régime's durability. By April 1653 the Rump's deficit was £700,000, or half its annual revenue. The Commonwealth was indeed 'an undischarged bankrupt' [161 *p. 82*].

This situation, which enfeebled the republic, was aggravated by the Dutch War. That war added greatly to the Rump's practical problems. The soldiers, feeling neglected, complained that what was spent so readily to improve the navy had been earmarked for the army. Some officers even suspected that the Rump had deliberately built up the navy as a political counterweight to the critical army [40]. Cromwell himself disliked a war against another Protestant power because it would weaken the fragile Protestant interest in Europe.

The Dutch War may have arisen from the Rumpers' concern with security against the royalists. The United Provinces offered a haven to cavaliers and active backing to Charles II. Long-standing trading and naval rivalries strengthened political antagonisms. In 1651, through a Navigation Act, the Rump contested the United Provinces' role as the entrepôt of the world and sought to capture for England some of the valuable trade hitherto carried by Dutch vessels. The contest with the Dutch for mastery of the seas and their traffic was continued by warfare. But the war was not universally liked. It was costly, it interrupted some trades and revealed gross incompetence in the running of the navy [97, 149, 158]. The soldiers objected that the war increased the Rump's tendency to postpone internal reforms and consumed the money which might have been spent on preachers, teachers, hospitals, workhouses and almshouses [126, 130].

In August 1652 the disgruntled officers listed their complaints, many familiar from 1647 and 1648. They wanted corrupt revenue officers dismissed and only godly magistrates to be continued. Parliament should contain 'only such as are pious and faithful to the interest of the Commonwealth': tests which would debar many Rumpers. Although the petition ranged over many other reforms, increasingly the officers were obsessed with three matters. The first was the question of the Rump passing power to a successor. The others were the reform of religion and the law.

The Rump, while not heedless of religious reform, seemed anxious to curtail religious liberty. A majority of MPs evidently favoured the retention of a national Church, which had broken down following the abolition of bishops, and wanted it to be financed in the traditional way by tithes* paid by the parishioners to their incumbents. In 1650 the Rump legislated against the more bizarre sects which had proliferated in the previous decade. Conservatives were disturbed because the fervent sectaries absented themselves from the local parish church, a practice helped by the Rump repealing the Act obliging regular attendance. Unlettered artisans, soldiers and even women worshipped and preached as they chose. Some belittled university qualifications and instead valued the promptings of the Holy Spirit, which any man or woman might feel and express. A few even questioned whether the Bible was the word of God and deserved the veneration usually accorded to it. Others, sure that they were among the elect destined for salvation, insisted that whatever they did they could commit no sin. The Rump's Blasphemy Act aimed at stopping those whose practices worked 'to the dissolution of all human society', and reassured many who had been affronted by the recent abuse of religious toleration [14, ii, *p. 410*; 46, 81].

The Adultery Act was similarly intended to check growing evils. It transferred to justices of the peace a job previously discharged by the now defunct church courts. The social consequences of adultery, such as the break-up of families and the begetting of bastards who burdened the parish rates, were unwelcome to local communities. In some areas magistrates were accustomed to proceeding against adulterers. The Rump's Act attempted to impose nationally the moral discipline which already existed in some towns and villages. The Adultery and Blasphemy Acts were more widely praised than reviled, and earned approval for the Rump. Yet the Acts proved difficult to enforce, since few in the counties would impose the stringent punishments [56, Thomas in 96, 183].

The godly criticised the Rump for failing to arrest the growth of irreligion and profanity. A bill to help propagate the gospel throughout the entire country was neglected by parliament. So too was a scheme presented to the Rump in 1652 by one of Cromwell's chaplains, John Owen. Owen suggested how to combine freedom for the respectable orthodox sects with control over the offensive groups, like the Catholics and Episcopalians on the one wing and the Ranters,* Seekers* and Anabaptists* on the other. The plan asked the state to supervise church affairs – a principle disputed by radical sectaries who wanted their congregations to have total autonomy. Local boards, empanelled by the state, would vet the qualifications and beliefs of those already in benefices and of those who aspired to preach. Those who scrupled could stay away from the parish church, but their alternative services would be overseen. Owen's plan, which carefully balanced freedom against discipline, did not commend itself to the Rump. Critics retorted that the Rump could neither provide orthodox Protestant preaching throughout its territories nor silence the unorthodox.

The Rumpers' alleged indifference to spreading godliness seemed to be confirmed in April 1653. The commissions for the propagation of the gospel in Wales and the north were due for renewal. The Welsh commission, though it had placed ministers and teachers in remote hamlets, was hated by some as an instrument of anglicisation. In practice it transferred power within Welsh communities to new groups [74]. The commission was also attacked for patronising religious fanatics who simply antagonised their congregations, and for misusing its funds. The Rump allowed the commissions to lapse. The decision offended both those, like Cromwell, who valued the commissions' spiritual achievements and those who had served as commissioners, most notably Major-General Thomas Harrison. The latter's influence over the Fifth Monarchists* and Cromwell was great, and was now thrown decisively against the Rump [62, 126].

The Rump's piecemeal efforts to reform the law disappointed those who had expected a more comprehensive programme. The disappointment mattered because those who wanted law reform included not only the army radicals but also those who regularly used the law courts, the landowners and merchants. Procedure was thought to be needlessly complicated, and the lawyers were reputed to be more concerned with maintaining their lucrative monopoly than in seeing fees regulated, obsolete laws repealed or procedure simplified. As the lawyers, especially the strong contingent in parliament, blocked change, the same crude anti-professionalism which was being directed against ordained and graduate clergy was turned on the legal profession [45, 111, 121, 143].

The Rump in December 1651 appointed a commission, chaired by the learned jurist, Matthew Hale, to review the entire legal system. The commission was to consider 'what inconveniences there are in the law; and how the mischiefs which grow for delays and charge-ableness and irregularites of the law may be prevented, and the speediest way to reform the same'. Within a year this sedulous body reported. It was alive to the dangers of introducing summary pro-cedures which might be arbitrary, or of repealing seemingly obsolete laws. It echoed the earlier radical requests that county courts and land registries be established in order that more cases could be settled locally and that the number of those about landownership could be reduced. The lawyer MPs prevented the recommendations becoming law. The lawyers rejoiced that they had averted the threat of change, but their behaviour added to the Rump's reputation for self-interest and inactivity.

The third issue on which the soldiery found the Rump wanting was the preparation of a new constitution. The Rump, like all parliaments touchy about its privileges, would not be dictated to. Yet it ignored the wishes of the army at its peril. The Rumpers' thoughts at first ran towards filling the vacant seats through by-elections. (Vacancies had been filled by this method in 1645–8.) But soon enough they turned to drafting a bill for a new representative. Past debates about a reformed parliament had concentrated on how the seats should be redistributed and how the members would be elected. Owing to the Rump's behaviour, two other problems complicated discussions. The Rump was very coy about naming the date of its own dissolution. With difficulty Cromwell stopped his officers in August 1652 from dictating the day when the Rump must end. At length, in the spring of 1653, the Rump itself announced that it would lay down power on 3 November 1653. The other problem was that in the unsettled state of the country, royalists were likely to win the elections. The Levellers had already faced this problem when they drafted constitutions, and had proposed that political rights should be limited to those who promised to exercise them responsibly. In practice this would mean testing political reliability. The Levellers would have done so by allowing only those who subscribed to their constitution to vote. It was inevitable that any new arrangements would debar, at least temporarily, those who opposed the revolution, and would involve scrutiny of the opinions of those elected.

The Rump, after delays, embodied its ideas in a bill by the spring of 1653. It accepted the arguments of many reformers and increased county representation at the expense of the less independent pocket boroughs. Thirty members each were assigned to the newly conquered countries of Ireland and Scotland. Turning to the franchise, the Rump substituted for the old forty-shilling freeholder qualification in the counties, which had admitted men of modest means to vote, a £200 property qualification. Although the franchise would be narrowed, the army commanders approved the proposal.

By April 1653 the Rump seemed to be preparing to transfer power. Cromwell had been right to tell his men to be patient and to trust the Rump. And yet, on 20 April 1653, when the Rump resumed debate on its bill for the new representative, Cromwell hastened to the Chamber and there angrily closed the sitting. In the past Cromwell's action has been explained as the result of the intolerable pressure from his soldiers, pressure which Cromwell could no longer resist because the Rump was about to pass a bill which would have perpetuated itself, and then to adjourn. Since the bill for the new representative does not survive, argument about its contents is necessarily conjectural. It has recently been suggested that what forced Cromwell to break with the Rump was not the fact that the latter intended simply to recruit new members to fill the vacant seats, but that in preparing to pass power to a completely new parliament the Rump had not been careful enough to guarantee that the new members would be men favourable to both the revolution and the army's objectives. It may be that the Rump itself proposed to reconvene on the eve of the new session in order to vet the new MPs' qualifications. If this were so, then the army might justifiably fear that the Rumpers would take a different, and laxer, view of what constituted good affection among the MPs. The soldiers suspected that the Rump would allow a parliament to come into existence which would promptly start dismantling what the revolution had so far achieved. When we recall the importance attached by the Levellers to the matter of vetting MPs' qualifications and the controversy which surrounded the question in the later parliaments of the Protectorate, it is plausible to suppose that the Rump's inadequate arrangements angered Cromwell and obliged him to act [126, 130].

If it was the prospect of a defective bill for a new representative suddenly being passed which decided Cromwell to dissolve the Rump, his decision has to be seen against growing dissatisfaction with the parliament. The Rump's failure to enact useful measures of legal and religious reform, and its eagerness to lavish scarce resources on a naval war, reluctantly made Cromwell believe the complaints current among his men, and act as they wanted. For all his love of parliamentary rule, Cromwell terminated it.

4 THE FIRST PHASE OF GODLY RULE: THE BAREBONES PARLIAMENT OF 1653

GODLY RULE

Pride's Purge, the king's execution and the army's triumphs raised to a new height hopes that England's protracted reformation was about to be completed. The Rump failed to make England into a godly nation. Now, from April 1653, Cromwell would try. The lethargic and increasingly ungodly Rump had been ejected. Thieves condemned to death were reprieved, suggesting that Cromwell agreed with those who criticised the laws which sentenced men to death for trivial offences, and wanted England's laws brought into conformity with the laws of God. He pleased Harrison and the radicals by renewing the commission for propagating the gospel in Wales, recently ended by the Rump [62, 126].

Soon Cromwell would summon to London an assembly which was designed to hasten the rule of the Saints* on earth, and would tell its members, 'you are at the edge of the promises and prophecies'. After temporising for months, Cromwell seemed to have allied with the Millenarians* who felt chosen by God to monopolise power and to dictate to their unregenerate countrymen how they should live. Cromwell had long shared the language and some of the dreams of the godly. Yet he now partnered these zealots partly because he believed their programme of intense moral regeneration would serve a useful political purpose. If we consider how Cromwell's opinions had evolved, we shall see why he reached this conclusion.

In 1640 when elected to the Long Parliament, Cromwell, the East Anglian squire, was little known outside the circle of Pym and Oliver St John. He was propelled to national fame by his proficiency as a cavalry commander. By 1645 he was a valued member of the parliamentary group which insisted that the Civil War must be won before terms could be discussed with the king. Cromwell was also moved to intervene more often in debate by his passionate belief in religious freedom. Having himself suffered from the prying enquiries of the

Laudian* clergy in the 1630s, he was dismayed when the Long Parliament curtailed the recently won religious liberty and tried instead to erect an exclusive and intolerant Presbyterian Church throughout England. Because he was the prominent patron of the religious sectaries, Cromwell was expected to embrace other radical causes. Some, such as the reform of the law or the better relief of the poor, he did support. But he did not want to tamper with existing hierarchies. His conservatism over the fate of the monarchy and the House of Lords and over franchise reform irritated radicals [63, 86].

Cromwell's opinions resembled those of many of his generation, who had matured in the early years of the century when the established Church and universities were clearly Calvinist,* when Protestantism had been threatened everywhere by resurgent popery and Arminianism,* and when the Stuarts sought to shake off the restraints imposed by parliaments. Cromwell desired a Church which was unambiguously Protestant in its theology and liturgy, vigorous in evangelising and manned by well-educated divines. He insisted that the state assist the Church in its work, and that at the parish level incumbents could rely on the aid of lay magistrates. He wanted to return the power which under the Stuarts had been concentrated in the hands of courtiers and their creatures to godly justices of the peace, constables and parish officials. Well-chosen magistrates would punish miscreants, order society carefully and instil moral discipline; men of the same type should also be returned to the periodic parliaments.

Much of Cromwell's thinking was similar to that of 'the middle group' – the loose alliance of reforming MPs who in the early 1640s had been guided by Pym and St John [86, 173]. Cromwell's conservative instincts made him approve reforms to overhaul badly functioning institutions. The clergy, for example, must be better paid and better educated if they were to overcome the widespread ignorance and irreligion. Ministers should be allowed to choose the ceremonies and beliefs which they followed, for it was foolish to lose the services of able men because they scrupled over minor points. Justices of the peace and jurors, if they were to govern and reform their districts, must be chosen and supervised more carefully. Parliament, if it was to work harmoniously with the government, needed to be regularly re-elected and to have members free from corrupting pressures and sensitive to the concerns of their godly constituents. Thus parliamentary seats would have to be re-distributed, and the frequency of elections and even the franchise itself might have to be modified. Furthermore, the permanent part of government, the successor of the Privy Council, would have to be more strictly controlled to make it better serve the nation.

Cromwell, unoriginal in his political thinking, left constitutional argument and the devising of new political arrangements to others – between 1647 and 1649 to his son-in-law, Ireton. What made Cromwell unusual, and set up a dangerous tension which made him veer wildly between apparently contradictory courses, was that he combined conventional political views with radical religious opinions. At first glance this combination may not seem odd. Cromwell was one of a sizeable minority of devout Calvinists of local standing who laboured in the early seventeenth century to establish godly rule in England. Educated by Calvinist schoolmasters, tutors and chaplains, reared on the nutritious myths of Foxe's *Book of Martyrs*, these men regarded the English as a chosen race, among whom the predicted reign of the saints on earth would first be accomplished. England would then effect that reconversion of the whole world, and Christ would come again [194, 195]. Convinced of their place in this divine plan, zealous landowners, merchants and magistrates employed grave tutors and chaplains in their households, and set a pattern of Christian behaviour for their children, servants and tenants. As churchwardens, overseers of the poor and justices of the peace they combated profanity and ungodliness and, through by-laws, enforced the stricter keeping of the Sabbath, outlawed blasphemy and checked drunkenness. In the 1630s the Laudian Church and Charles I's Privy Council sided with the unregenerate and undid much of the Calvinists' work by reviving profane entertainments and by hampering the godly magistrates [56, 168].

The champions of moral reformation craved a government which would abet and not obstruct their programme. In 1640 they thought they had one in the Long Parliament. But until 1649 godly reformation, though talked of in parliament, had to wait on the political settlement of the country. When ungodly forces were dramatically overthrown, with parliament purged and monarchy and the House of Lords abolished, the atmosphere became electric with expectations. Great changes, unthought of a few years earlier, had occurred. Surely more must follow. Those who with a naïve literalism scanned the Bible found in the prophecies of the Book of Revelations the key to what must happen, and agitated to hasten the process. Others, more modestly, saw a chance to achieve social amelioration and moral improvement. Some of the Rump's Acts, against blasphemy and adultery, spreading the gospel in the north and Wales, and bringing Scotland and Ireland to heel, delighted the godly. Moreover the godly

were favoured now as they had not been since the 1620s. Manning
local and national government, they enforced neglected social and
moral laws and edged the unregenerate English nearer to godliness
[69, 103, 148].

Cromwell believed that God had given clear signs that the time had
arrived to speed godly regeneration, and that he and his army had
been singled out as vital helpers in that process. If God's injunctions
were now disregarded, the English would call down divine wrath on
themselves. But Cromwell also shrewdly endorsed the godly programme because it would achieve political stability. Thereby he
inverted the usual wisdom that only after political normality had
returned to the country could godly reformation be inaugurated.

In 1653, he dearly wanted to revive customary political processes,
and to base government on the people's consent expressed freely in
elections. Yet he hesitated to hold elections lest they return royalists
and enemies of the revolution rather than disinterested reformers.
Cromwell's vision of England as a godly nation would remain a del-
usive mirage if he had to wait until quiet settled over the country. The
alternative was to enforce a godly dictatorship forthwith. The actual
process of imposing this rule, as well as its results, would begin the
transformation. Godly rulers would prise men away from their
corrupt and lazy habits, and simultaneously spread the benefits of a
just government. The law would be improved and cheapened, scarce
foodstuffs would be allocated equitably, trickery at markets would be
eliminated by the stricter use of correct weights and measures, servile
obligations of tenants towards their masters would be ended, the
poor, widows and orphans would be better treated and the un-
employed found work. Experience of godly rule would soon open
men's eyes to its excellence, and stop them longing for the exiled
Stuarts. As the English people were transformed, so they would
conform to the new political system. Of course realists could foresee
problems, notably the tenacity with which the ungodly would cling to
their present, easy-going existence. Cromwell, however, brushed aside
objections and, in April 1653, opened a period of godly rule, which
would bring political as well as ideological satisfaction.

THE CALLING OF THE BAREBONES PARLIAMENT

No one had intervened to save the Rump. In its last months Fifth
Monarchists had spat venom at it. So too had Presbyterian preachers,
powerful in some London parishes, and affronted first by the murder
of the king, then by the Rump's failure to impose a national

Presbyterian system. Efforts by the Rump to identify its critics and to exclude them from all influential posts by tendering to them an oath of engagement to the new order proved ineffective and divisive. Royalists, contrary to the Rump's intention, had sworn the Engagement while entering mental reservations that the government they were prepared to uphold was the one which ought to rule and not the one actually ruling. Presbyterians, in contrast, had publicly debated whether or not to take the oath, and in the end many had refused [3, 92]. Those few who regretted the Rump's passing and who would scheme for its return were mainly its members and employees. The danger from the former Rumpers, or Commonwealthmen, would grow, not because the cause was popular, but because they were adept at exploiting provincial dislike of any central government. As yet, however, their opposition was in the future.

Cromwell, having removed the remnant of the parliament legally elected in 1640, had to find a replacement which would win the affections of the people and unify the country. But Cromwell had apparently fallen under the sway of two groups with little following in the nation, the millenarians and the radical army officers. Major-General Harrison, the link between the army and the Fifth Monarchists, had advised Cromwell to be rid of the Rump, and now, high in Cromwell's esteem, was well placed to influence events.

In April 1653 authority had passed temporarily to a council of army officers and a new, smaller Council of State, seven of whose ten members were soldiers. Cromwell wanted the godly part of the nation, acting as a constituent assembly, to devise the settlement which first the Long Parliament and then the Rump had delayed. The difficulty was to assemble, in an atmosphere still generally inimical to reform, a group of men who could at once claim to represent the nation and who would institute reformation. The army council discussed various expedients. Cromwell was attracted to the suggestion of rule by a collection of godly men. Harrison, coached by the Millenarians and certain that the answer lay in Scripture, proposed an assembly of seventy, modelled on the Jewish Sanhedrin. Cromwell preferred a larger body, and in the end he carried the day: one hundred and forty would be summoned to frame a new settlement [126].

While the Council of Officers debated, unsolicited advice reached it. Scattered congregations and individual preachers, encouraged by Cromwell's apocalyptic language, bombarded him and the officers with projects. They asked that lawyers and Presbyterians, the two groups often blamed for the Rump's poor record, be debarred from future parliaments [*Doc. 6*]. They demanded that ungodly institutions, including the law courts, the universities and the tithes which paid ministers, should go. Some even asked that the Jews be re-admitted to England, thereby fulfilling the prophecy that only after the reconversion of the Jews would Christ come again [41].

Once the decision to call an assembly had been taken, Cromwell and the officers had to agree a method of selecting suitable members. Part of the problem was to identify reliable men in the counties. The commission of the peace, the usual channel through which such information was relayed to the central government, was being thoroughly purged. The new JPs had little grip over their regions, and could not be trusted to suggest nominees. An alternative source of information was the separatist congregations, the obvious centres of godliness. Some were canvassed, especially those in Wales known to Harrison; others volunteered advice. Occasionally, as in Suffolk, Kent and Wales, some of the suggestions were adopted. More often the officers used their own, sometimes inaccurate, local knowledge to pick the members of the assembly. Some nominees were out of sympathy with the officers, and the choice inadequately represented the entire British Isles [126].

Those who ridiculed the nominated members as 'no better than attorneys, tanners, wheelwrights and the meanest sort of mechanics', and depicted the radical London tradesman Praise-God Barebone as the typical member, allowed prejudice to distort their analyses. Those selected were generally modest gentlemen whose horizons were bounded by their parish rather than their county, merchants and small-town lawyers who before 1640 could not have expected to sit in parliament. They were typical of the men who had come forward to serve parliament in the 1640s. Having contributed to parliament's victory, they now shared the rewards. One defect of the assembly, not seen as such when it opened, was the lack of previous parliamentary experience among its members. This was offset by widespread local administrative experience. Most had served as assessment commissioners and 119 as JPs. Nor was the assembly free of those partisans, the lawyers and the Presbyterians, whom some of the Saints had wanted to exclude. The majority was an unknown quantity, at first likely to be unversed in procedure and unknown to each other. For Cromwell the members' political innocence was peculiarly attractive, for it increased his hopes of a biddable assembly [188].

Cromwell opened the nominated assembly, soon to be known as the Barebones Parliament, with great optimism on 4 July 1653. Immediately the members voted, against Cromwell's wishes, to assume the title of a Parliament. In doing so they laid claim to the privileges and powers traditionally enjoyed by a parliament, and which Cromwell, after his experiences with the Rump, had wanted to deny them. Cromwell had conceived the gathering as a constituent assembly which would draft a constitution and then retire; the members saw themselves as partners in a government already established. When we remember the comparative inexperience of most members, this first sign of self-confidence, soon followed by a spate of legislation, is surprising, and has led to praise of the parliament. A number of measures drafted and discussed by the Rump were hurried onto the statute book. The assembly speedily organised ten standing committees to prepare new bills. Acts passed included further improvements in the law, by helping poor debtors, by preventing judgments on narrowly technical grounds and by removing fees for original writs. Steps were taken to eliminate corruption in the much expanded central revenue departments. Civil marriage was instituted – another breach in the state Church's monopoly and an extra burden on overworked magistrates. The registering of births, marriages and deaths was improved, so that more accurate details would aid those dispensing poor relief. In Ireland, lands confiscated from the Catholic rebels were bestowed on the soldiers who had served there and on civilians who had earlier paid for the island's reconquest. Parliament took over nominating the Council of State, enlarged to about thirty members. Unfortunately the members in addition turned to the same controversial matters which had embittered relations between the Rump and the army [126].

PARLIAMENT DISSOLVED

Cromwell's invitation to selected Saints to gather in London unleashed pent-up mysticism, millenarianism, and hatred of ancient rivals. New and violent attacks endangered the state's continuing supervision of the Church, tithes, the universities, the law courts and the Inns of Court where lawyers were trained. Yet fervent Millenarians, the Fifth Monarchists and Baptists, intent on rooting up immediately all corrupt institutions, numbered at most a dozen in parliament. However, they enjoyed a disproportionate influence, in part because they attended diligently and steered key committees. Also, on occasion, they were supported by others who, while not sharing the Millenarians' vision of future society, nevertheless wanted the shameful abuses in the Church and law remedied.

Some contemporaries suspected that Cromwell, for all his enthusiastic talk of regeneration, had priorities very different from those of the radicals. He wanted 'the continuance of our ancient laws under settled magistrates and an ordered ministry of learned and able divines bred at the universities, [and] to bring the stream of government to run much in the old channel'. When he realised how parliament was jeopardising those ideals, he let it end. These differences of approach showed most starkly when parliament turned to legal and ecclesiastical changes.

Tithes were the first controversial issue to be debated. On 19 July their fate was referred to a committee. The matter was a complicated one which had already generated acrimonious discussion, and would do so again. Moderate reformers contended that tithes undermined schemes for a more effective preaching ministry. Tithes varied greatly in yield and often gave an incumbent an inadequate income. Collecting tithes could produce unseemly squabbles. Others maintained that tithes burdened the poor, who saw a tenth of their produce grabbed by the clergy. Fundamentalists alleged that tithes lacked proper biblical sanction. One reason why tithes had escaped abolition was the lack of a suitable replacement. An alternative would be for the state to pay all approved ministers from a central treasury; another would be for ministers to rely on the voluntary offerings of their congregations. State payment had recently been introduced in Wales and Ireland, but worked only while the number of clergymen was small and while the income from tithes was supplemented from other official revenues. A fund from which ministers could be paid might have been created when the Rump confiscated its enemies' estates. But instead the money had been spent on government. The state could do no more than augment very low stipends, and leave the majority of the beneficed clergy to live on tithes. Voluntary contributions had been paid to many sectarian preachers throughout the 1640s. But any national use of this method was opposed on the grounds that ministers would be maintained only where the godly were prepared to pay. Since the godly were still sparsely scattered, especially outside the towns, many districts would be denied the regular services of preachers. Furthermore the parishioners, being the paymasters, could call the tune played by their ministers, and might frustrate any rigorous reformation [86, 108, 169, 181].

The question was further complicated by some 3,000 laymen owning tithes, as a result of acquiring monastic lands in the sixteenth century. These lay impropriators, unwilling to lose a useful income, were likely to oppose the abolition of tithes unless they were compensated. On 17 November the radicals in parliament carried a motion to end the laity's right to present ministers to livings. On 2 December the committee reported to the House how the Church should be organised. It endorsed, while modifying, Owen's scheme of 1652. Government-appointed commissioners would eject and choose ministers, who would still be maintained by tithes. The Fifth Monarchists and other voluntaryists, who wanted each congregation to remain independent, condemned continuing state supervision. On 10 December the radicals challenged the committee's report and defeated by two votes the first of its recommendations. This presaged the abolition of tithes. Cromwell, who believed that the state should shield the Church against the prevailing ungodliness and indifference, feared the overthrow of traditionally organised religion.

The radicals had been supported by MPs who, as a matter of tactics, voted for dramatic changes in the hope of precipitating the long-delayed reforms. For the same reason equally radical motions for law reform were carried in the Barebones Parliament. MPs, assisted by some members and the proposals of Hale's committee, were determined to tackle this tricky matter. In August 1653, a second and more militant parliamentary committee started to codify the laws, with the aim of reducing the many volumes of statutes and cases 'into the bigness of a pocket book'. Obsolete laws would be repealed, those which conflicted with reason or the laws of God would be adjusted, and penalties would be fitted to crimes so that men were no longer hanged for theft. Reformers had long planned to distil the essence of the law and knew it had been done recently in some North American colonies. However, some opposed the scheme for 'a new body' of law because England, an advanced and populous trading society, required a complex collection of laws. If the laws were summarily simplified, many injured parties might be left without any adequate legal remedy. It was also feared that the doctrinaire might dominate this second committee, and either sweep away numerous essential laws or decreee draconian penalties, particularly for moral peccadilloes, on the basis of Old Testament authority. In the event, the committee had not finished its work before the parliament closed.

Plans were made for the hated court of Chancery. Because it dealt with property and mortgage disputes, Chancery was much used by landowners. In the sixteenth century it had won a reputation for fairness and celerity which lingered long after it had become clogged with business. By the 1640s 23,000 cases were said to be pending in

Chancery. The problem was clear, but not the cure. Radical MPs suggested that the court be abolished before the autumn law term opened. A majority agreed on 5 August that only Chancery's outright abolition would induce the authorities to substitute an alternative, simplified procedure. Once the motion to abolish Chancery had been passed, radicals and moderates discovered that they had meant different things by it. The radicals expected the court to be suspended immediately; the moderates regarded the motion as a declaration of intent and insisted that Chancery continue until its replacement was ready. The radicals, knowing that Chancery would disappear only when an alternative had been devised, prepared a bill which would substitute a summary and cheap procedure. This bill had not emerged from the committee before parliament ended. Self-interested lawyers and office-holders in Chancery may have delayed its progress [45, 121, 126].

By November 1653 the Barebones Parliament alternated between radical and conservative motions. Cromwell was disillusioned. The parliament was not settling or reforming the country as smoothly as he had expected. Part of the fault lay with Cromwell. After his opening exhortations to the members he had failed to put in managers or spell out his programme. He was true to his long-standing belief that parliament should be independent and free from interference by the executive [86]. Neither Cromwell nor Lambert, though co-opted into the assembly, attended. Without guidance, the Barebones Parliament tended to go where the radicals blew. For their part, the radicals were disappointed by Cromwell and particularly by his attitude towards the Dutch War. Cromwell wanted to end it; the Fifth Monarchists urged that the advantage which had been so painfully achieved should be used to beat the Dutch into surrender. By November 1653 the Millenarians openly called Cromwell 'a man of sin, the old dragon and many other scripture ill names', and regarded him as a worse enemy than the Rump had ever been [41, 97].

As Cromwell watched parliament's activities, he feared that the radicals might triumph and destroy many familiar institutions. Ominously, the tax base of the régime – the excise – was questioned. Also the close balance within the House made the future uncertain. He had expected the Barebones Parliament to continue until November 1654, and was reluctant to dissolve it prematurely. As so often, he let others act for him. The vote of 10 December which endangered the state Church and tithes precipitated action. The conservatives who had retaliated against radical motions and had defended Chancery and tithes consulted some army officers, and then went early to the Chamber and surrendered their powers to Cromwell.

This first experiment in godly rule had ended ignominiously. How much parliament's activities had been observed outside London is impossible to gauge. It may have been blamed for the thorough purge of local government conducted in its name in the summer of 1653. Although the changes varied in extent from county to county, Buckinghamshire, Surrey, Devon, Yorkshire and Hereford are known to have been seriously affected. The few gentlemen of substance who had continued in the commission of the peace, despite all the recent upheavals, disappeared. They were replaced, sometimes by zealots, more frequently by compliant nonentities. The worst offence of these new justices of the peace was that they belonged to a type – parochial gentry, traders, attorneys and busy officials – never before employed in running the shires. Those whom they had displaced inevitably derided a régime which had to use such men. In general these novice magistrates lacked the local standing and connections to make them effective county governors, and so they could do little to establish the régime in the provinces [24, 43, 56, 69]. Yet these local agents did not always accurately reflect the outlook of the masters in Westminster, and as a result may have blunted the local impact of an unpopular order [31, 83, 115, 118].

Only the Chancery lawyers, jubilant that 'their great Diana' had been spared, lit bonfires and caroused when the Barebones Parliament ended. Most of their countrymen waited apprehensively to see what novelty would next be produced. Power had been returned to Cromwell and his army, and any reversion to normal government seemed more remote than ever.

5 THE FIRST PHASE OF HEALING AND SETTLING: THE PROTECTORATE

THE INSTRUMENT OF GOVERNMENT

Cromwell, having glimpsed the unpopularity of godly dictatorship when exercised by the Barebones Parliament and how it unsettled the country, turned to more conventional policies. The problems of finding a way to govern the nation and win support, urgent in 1649, required an immediate solution by the end of 1653. Cromwell, although not abandoning reform, let it wait on political reconciliation: healing divisions and settling the government definitively.

As we have already emphasised, Cromwell lacked the inventiveness to frame constitutional schemes himself. He felt the absence of Ireton, who had died in Ireland in 1651, for Ireton had shared his essential traditionalism. Almost indiscriminately Cromwell used the proposals first of his army colleagues and then of civilians who kept alive some of the ideals of the old parliamentary middle group. In April 1653 he had heeded Major-General Harrison. In December 1653 he listened to a more conservative general, John Lambert, probably the most influential officer in the forces after Cromwell. As the Barebones Parliament argued, Lambert planned what might replace it. Thus within four days of the Barebones Parliament abdicating, Cromwell had accepted Lambert's constitution, the Instrument of Government [126, 163].

The Instrument combined many earlier proposals, ranging from the terms Pym had demanded from the king in 1641 and 1642, through the army's suggestions of 1647 and 1648, to the devices of the Rump. The haste with which it had been stitched together was shown by its omissions and ambiguities. The trivial jostled the essential. The Instrument subscribed to the current orthodoxy of the sovereign people, but, like other recent arrangements, treated the people as too fickle as yet to be allowed the free exercise of their sovereignty. For the moment the people's powers were assumed by a triumvirate of unequal partners. A Protector, a Council of State and an occasional, single-chamber parliament replaced the three traditional elements of king, Privy Council and Lords and Commons gathered in Parliament [163]. The office of Protector was conferred on Cromwell for life. His successor would be selected by the Council of State. The Protector enjoyed many of the powers previously vested in the monarch, such as conferring honours, appointing magistrates and pardoning the convicted. However, his more substantial powers had to be shared either with parliament or, more often, with the Council of State. Although certain unique rights were conferred on the Protector, notably the obligation to annul any proposed measures which would overturn the fundamental principles of the Instrument, they were too imprecisely defined to be exercised easily.

Recent observation of how parliament had abused its authority and the realisation that parliament alone could never guarantee satisfactory government, led to a subordinate role being assigned to the assembly. The chief watchdog would be the Council of State, a revised version of the old Privy Council and Pym's projects. The Council of State differed from earlier schemes in being less easily controlled by parliament than Pym had wanted and in being more powerful. In all matters of policy and administration it was to guide the Protector. It would nominate Cromwell's successor and, for much of the time, would recruit its own members. Parliamentary surveillance was confined to the periods when parliament was sitting (five months in every three years), and to submitting lists of candidates from which the existing councillors could choose new colleagues, and then to supplying seven members of a committee of sixteen which would investigate complaints against councillors.

The Council would at most number twenty-one. Fifteen councillors were named in the Instrument. Thereafter new appointments were rare, and made when parliament was not in session. Vacancies occurred through death or voluntary resignation; no one was removed after a parliamentary enquiry. Cromwell complained of the restraints imposed on him as Protector by the Council. Evidence about discussions in the Council is scanty, though we do know of divergences over foreign policy. Cromwell absented himself from 60 per cent of the recorded meetings. However, the circumstances in which the Council had been chosen, the identity of its members and the personality of the Protector all made it likely that the councillors would usually defer to him. The councillors, better administrators than politicians, drew on local experiences before they had been called to their present, high places. In addition they were assisted by skilled civil servants [155].

The new constitution gave parliament a role little better than it had had under the king and certainly less powerful than that which the Rump had enjoyed. Parliament, as had been enacted in 1641, must automatically assemble every three years, and sit at least five months. In the hope of making it more independent and representative, its composition was changed, along the lines planned by the Rump. County seats were reallocated, roughly in proportion with the tax burden, and increased to two-thirds of the total of 400. This increase was at the expense of the supposedly corrupt and unduly deferential borough constituencies. Scotland and Ireland were assigned thirty members each: too few to protect adequately their national interests against English hostility, but sufficient to convince the Protector's opponents that they provided Cromwell with a solid block of supporters.

The franchise permanently excluded Catholics and participants in the Irish rebellion of 1641. Active English royalists would be debarred from voting in the next three elections so that the new régime would be secured and they could be cured of their animosity. The borough franchise, which varied from virtually all adult male inhabitants to a tight clique of office-holders, was unaltered. In the counties, now the predominant element in the House, the franchise suggested by the Rump, a £200 per annum property qualification, was adopted. Merchants and traders whose wealth was in movable goods entered the electorate for the first time, but many modest men who, as forty-shilling freeholders, had hitherto voted were now disenfranchised. The scheme, by limiting the vote to men of substance, may well have been intended to increase further the independence of parliament by reducing opportunities for landlord pressure on poor voters. It has been estimated that it reduced the county electorate to a mere third of its pre-war size [89]. Another question, which became acute after the election of the first Protectorate Parliament, was how to vet members' qualifications. In the early seventeenth century, MPs' sensitivity on this issue embittered relations with the executive. The prospect of inadequate controls over new MPs had caused the rift between Cromwell and the Rump. The Instrument of Government stipulated that only those of known integrity, fearing God and of good conversation should be returned as MPs. Also all MPs should undertake not to tamper with the central principle of the new settlement, the division of power between the Protector and parliament. But the Instrument did not specify who should impose these imprecise tests, and so stored up trouble for the future.

Former Rumpers disliked the limited power entrusted to parliament in the matters hotly disputed in the past, such as control of the executive, the armed forces, finances and the Church. Another serious defect of the Instrument lay in the question of whether, or how, it could be revised. Cromwell evidently regarded it as sacrosanct, and conflict would arise when parliament took the settlement to pieces [*Doc. 9*]

In financial matters the Instrument distinguished, but without enough care, between the ordinary and exceptional costs of government. The Protector and Council were empowered to use the customs and other revenues of their choice to maintain an army of 30,000, the navy and the civil administration. They were also allowed to raise money for special needs before parliament met. At the same time, the Instrument decreed that 'no tax, charge or imposition' could be 'laid on the people but by common consent in Parliament'. On closer scrutiny parliament discovered that the occasions when it was likely to control taxation were rare. There were weaknesses in the terms on which the army was controlled. The traditional fighting force, the militia,* was subjected to the Protector and Council in the intervals between parliaments, and to the Protector and parliament at other times. The standing forces, of late grown to over 57,000, were also to be governed by the Protector and parliament when the latter was in being. Whether by accident or design, nothing was said of the standing army when parliament was not meeting, so that the Protector could assume that it was his to do with as he wished.

In religion the Instrument sought to balance toleration and control. As Cromwell desired, the state retained care for seeing that Christianity was practised, and continued to pay ministers with tithes until a less vexatious method could be found. Deviant sects would be tolerated so long as they did not disturb the peace, adhere to popery or episcopacy, or behave licentiously. The Protector was authorised to annul any laws proposed by parliament which jeopardised liberty of conscience.

THE FIRST MONTHS OF THE PROTECTORATE

Until parliament assembled in September 1654, Cromwell as Protector, helped by the Council of State, could rule the country as he wanted. Critics alleged that his whole career had been directed to this outcome. Cromwell passionately denied any personal ambition, and insisted that only his sense of public duty and his obligations to God and God's people made him accept the onerous office.

Cromwell's urgent tasks were, as the Rump's and the Barebones' had been, to still criticism and to win backing. Cromwell was most seriously threatened by former colleagues, some of whom felt betrayed by his assumption of supreme power. Millenarians railed against him as an apostate. Quickly their leader, Harrison, was stripped of his commission and forced into rural retirement. The Leveller gadfly Lilburne denounced the Protectorate and was hustled away to prison in the Channel Islands. Although sectarian critics might sting the régime, they were unlikely to destroy it.

More important were the attitudes of the soldiery and the officeholders. At the moments of choice in 1647, 1648 and 1653 Cromwell had sided with the soldiers. On becoming Protector, though it was at the behest of the army, he was thought by some officers to have deserted the cause for which they had fought throughout the 1640s. The army in Ireland was particularly restless. As a matter of deliberate policy some of the most radical officers had been shipped there in 1649. Radicals deeply entrenched themselves in the high command and Dublin administration. Ludlow, a friend of the Commonwealthmen and both a civil governor and commander in Dublin, openly challenged the Protectorate in 1654 by resigning his civil post rather than accept the new constitution [18, 34]. The pusillanimous reaction of the Commander-in-Chief and civil governor, Charles Fleetwood (Cromwell's son-in-law), let disaffection infect the entire English garrison. Restless officers in other parts of the British Isles also alarmed Cromwell. Although his ultimate aim was to rest his régime on civilian followers, the latter would be won over only slowly, and until then he needed a dependable army.

In addition Cromwell worried whether the rich London merchants would lend money to the impoverished régime, and whether officeholders would serve under the new order. The City, though cool, was not openly obstructive. Too many of its privileges derived from the central government for the corporation openly to oppose the Protectorate. Lawyers questioned the legality of the Instrument, and some judges resigned. However, enough judges were persuaded to man the courts, some of them men of distinction like Matthew Hale, for the administration of justice to continue. Those employed by the state, whether in the London bureaucracy or in local government, were seldom eager to sacrifice their careers for awkward scruples. Cromwell, by substituting for the Rump's Engagement a much less exacting test, widened the circle from which the government's servants could be drawn [33]. His intention, as yet stated only tentatively, was to efface the quarrels of the past and instead accept the help of anyone well affected to the present government. He hoped to win over the leading families, most of whom had retired from public life under the Long Parliament or Rump. The policy was hazardous. Many gentry could not forget how they had been treated in the 1640s, nor would they alter their allegiances and support the novel régime. If Cromwell readmitted such men to local office, he risked undermining the Protectorate, for few of the old county governors shared his vision of a reformed society [117].

Installed as Protector, Cromwell went seriously to work. His days were spent usually at St James's Palace or in the precincts of Whitehall, with weekends sometimes passed at Hampton Court [109]. Modestly he assumed some of the trappings of majesty, mindful that foreign emissaries had to be impressed. Inevitably he lost touch with the provinces in which he had originated and, to a lesser extent, with the army in which his triumphant career had been built.

Troubles in Scotland and Ireland had to be dealt with. Scotland felt the costs of English occupation more than the benefits of union. The new systems of law, land tenure and religious toleration pleased only a minority. The traditional leaders of Scottish society, the nobles, lairds and Presbyterian ministers, were affronted by their loss of control. By 1653 the royalists, led by Lord Glencairn, had rekindled resistance in parts of the Highlands. Within a year the trouble had spread into the Lowlands and was being fomented by some Presbyterian ministers. There was again the danger that Scotland would serve as a base for the Stuarts. In April 1654 Cromwell sent a new commander, George Monck, to crush the disorders. His campaign was backed by concessions to win over waverers and by intensified reform which might create a solid Cromwellian party on which the Protectorate could base itself in Scotland [49].

Cromwell, alarmed by the news of unrest in Ireland, sent his younger son, Henry, to assess the situation. Henry Cromwell blamed the spread of disaffection in the army and government there on the indulgence of Fleetwood towards all who professed godliness. Cromwell ignored his son's unsentimental advice to dismiss Fleetwood and other malcontents. Instead he speeded the island's resettlement in the hope that military rule could be phased out. The estates of the defeated Catholics were slowly allocated to English soldiers and investors. This would extend the policy of plantation, successfully adopted in Ulster and Munster earlier in the century, and strengthen the Protestant interest there [135].

Simultaneously reform was inaugurated in England. The plan of the Barebones Parliament to bring all official receipts into a single treasury was carried out. Cromwell and his Council then returned to reforming Chancery. Cromwell demonstrated his moderation by consulting the legal profession. When it offered no proposals, he resurrected the scheme of the Hale Commission, and used it as the basis for his ordinance of August 1654. This moderate measure kept the court, but abolished unnecessary offices, simplified procedure, regulated fees to stop overcharging, ended queue-jumping and forbade the sale of offices. The modesty of the changes, aimed at making a sound institution function properly, dismayed the few who had campaigned for Chancery's total destruction, and yet failed to appease the self-interested lawyers. All too quickly the Chancery lawyers nullified the reform. They would persuade the 1654 parliament to suspend the ordinance. Then in 1655 the commissioners instructed to apply the new procedures refused, and instead used the old. Only by appointing new commissioners did Cromwell secure nominal compliance. But in 1658 the Chancery Ordinance was allowed to lapse [33, 89].

Cromwell also dusted down the scheme for ecclesiastical reform originally offered to the Rump by Owen in 1652. The principles of a state-controlled Church, supported for the moment by tithes, and of limited toleration outside it, had been written into the Instrument. The state established a board of commissioners in London (the triers) to scrutinise a minister's credentials before he was inducted into a benefice. Cromwell did not wish the triers to enquire minutely into a man's beliefs, and hoped that a broadly-sketched list of fundamental Christian tenets could be agreed which might then be used as a test. Until such a document could be compiled, he made sure that varied opinions – of Presbyterians, Independents* and even Baptists – were represented among the triers, so that all worthy ministers could be admitted to preach. As well as the central board, commissioners in each county were to eject clergy and schoolmasters unsound in doctrine, politics or way of life. These local bodies, which included laymen, may have protected favoured ministers from deprivation and subjected others to vendettas. It tended to be godly dictators in London who foisted on the localities clergymen of their, and not the parishioners', choosing. Understandably the godly praised this system, but the majority attached still to the old liturgy disliked it. The survival of familiar parish worship, little altered by recent decrees, was assisted by continuity in the personnel of the Church. Only 28 per cent of parishes, concentrated in the south-east, had their incumbents ejected [85, 86, 89].

Cromwell revived schemes to make the Church a more effective evangelist by making better use of its resources. Since the late 1640s some of the revenue seized by the state from the old Anglican hierarchy had been used to augment poor clergymen's stipends and to create lecturerships to replace the abolished cathedral clergy. The trustees for the maintenance of ministers, established first in 1650, were brought directly under the Protector's control, and had their annual budget increased to £50,000. They hoped to pay every minister in England at least £100 per annum The Protector also resumed the Rump's work of dividing and uniting parishes. The present spread of parishes and churches no longer corresponded with the seventeenth-century distribution of population. Change was difficult, because orders for union or division had to be promoted at Whitehall. Not only did a parish need highly-placed friends to put its case; it might need much money with which to compensate a lay patron for the loss of his rights over a parish about to disappear or to pay for the building of a new church. Alterations occurred slowly and patchily.

Cromwell also patronised the universities. Oxford and Cambridge, crammed with apologists of the Stuarts and bishops, had been remodelled drastically in the late 1640s. Cromwell violently resisted those who argued that the universities must be swept away in preparation for the millennium. He took pains to appoint grave and orthodox divines as heads of colleges and as professors because he believed that well-governed universities would produce Calvinist graduates who within a generation would staff the ministry and local and national administration. If Cromwell viewed the colleges primarily as Puritan seminaries, he also knew that a godly élite would assist his political plans for reforming and stabilising England.

Much remained to be done as parliament approached: the criminal law was untouched, and no confession of faith had been promulgated. Nevertheless the reforms of 1654 merit their description as 'the great series of reforming ordinances' [33 *p. 47*], and showed that Cromwell had not abandoned reform, even when much occupied with security and foreign affairs.

Cromwell's diplomatic successes must be seen against a background of European conflict. France warred with Spain; Sweden wrestled with Denmark for dominance in the Baltic. It was not difficult for England to profit from this situation, when her aid was eagerly sought. The critics of James I's and Charles I's timid policies, on assuming power after 1649, ruthlessly asserted England's interests in Europe. War became an instrument of policy, as the Dutch War showed. Cromwell believed that everywhere a resurgent popery threatened Protestantism. The intrigues of the royalists, whether in

England, Scotland, Ireland or Europe, fitted into this design for universal dominion.

By April 1654 Cromwell had ended the Duch War. In the following months England concluded trading treaties with Sweden, a vital source of naval supplies, and with Portugal. At the same time Cromwell and his Council weighed the arguments for a Spanish or French alliance. Cromwell searched for an economical use for the navy, so recently and expensively overhauled. He was greatly taken with the notion of a naval war against Spain, notwithstanding the contrary arguments from Lambert and the cloth merchants. He thought it would pay for itself if the treasure fleet could be captured, and contended that traditional commercial, strategic and religious objectives would be advanced. He proposed to send the bulk of the fleet into the Mediterranean, where it might harass pirates, overawe rivals and impress potential allies (notably the French) while a smaller expedition sailed to the West Indies to capture the Spanish island of Hispaniola [97, 122, 171].

THE FIRST PROTECTORATE PARLIAMENT

Cromwell believed that his reforming record would please his countrymen when they voted for a new parliament. But the elections in July 1654 were the first full ones since 1640, and inevitably allowed accumulated grievances to be expressed. The régime for its own safety debarred known opponents from voting. Cromwell's reforms as yet had made little positive impact and no systematic propaganda had persuaded a sullen electorate of the merits of the novel government. In the counties, now returning two-thirds of the MPs, uncertainty as to who could vote under the new £200 property qualification was rife, and probably meant that the qualifications were not strictly observed.

Even had Cromwell so wished, it would have been difficult to influence the outcome of the elections. His régime was ill-informed about provincial opinion; the number of candidates amenable to his wishes was small; the county seats were traditionally less easily guided by the executive. But Cromwell did not want to tamper with parliament's independence; he had approved the alterations in the franchise and the increase in county membership in order to obtain an assembly free from corrupt influences. His ideal remained a freely elected parliament, for the moment chosen on a much restricted franchise, which would voluntarily co-operate with him. Accordingly he did little to direct either the elections or the parliament once it had opened [114].

Most voters and MPs disliked the Protectorate both as a constitutional hybrid invented by the soldiery, and as the powerful central government. The effects of a Cromwellian Protectorate were similar to, though usually worse than, those of Stuart monarchy. High taxes consumed wealth and beggared the poor; centralisation robbed the localities of the chance to order their own affairs; and only those with access to Cromwell and his entourage enjoyed local or national offices. Cromwell, having reluctantly assumed some of the characteristics of a monarch, visibly projected a court ethos against which country gentlemen could rail. Politics again exhibited the ambiguous revulsion against, and attraction towards, the powerful executive which had been their chief feature before the Civil War. Cromwell could at least comfort himself with the fact that the majority of MPs wanted to amend rather than overthrow the Protectorate, particularly by returning more power to the counties.

In 1654, as in earlier parliaments, the apolitical majority whose political service was limited to membership of the Barebones Parliament or local office and who regarded attendance at Westminster as an irksome chore, were whipped and led. The veterans of the Long Parliament, especially the Rumpers, played upon provincial worries and organised the inchoate hostility towards the Protectorate. About 125 MPs in 1654 had sat in the Long Parliament, and it was they, led by Arthur Haselrig, Thomas Scot, John Birch and John Bradshaw, who directed the new assembly. Only when they had taken their seats did these veterans unveil their alternative to the Protectorate: a sovereign parliament, unlikely to be more loved than the Rump itself. From among the novices who formed the majority of MPs, some of whom had been royalists in the 1640s, there gradually emerged men willing to contest with the Commonwealthmen for the leadship of the House. MPs like Anthony Ashley Cooper, Sir Charles Wolseley and Lord Broghill, young and open-minded, were prepared to tinker with the Protectorate, seeing it as a fresh version of the old balanced constitution, until it worked well.

Though Cromwell was disturbed to hear that Commonwealthmen had been elected, he approached the parliament with his habitual optimism. He defended his own actions as Protector and warned the MPs against the extravagances of the Barebones Parliament. He expected the new parliament to avoid the snares set by royalists, Catholics, foreign conspirators, Levellers and Fifth Monarchists, and instead to reform England. He believed that the nation lay at the 'entrances and doors of hope', and expected MPs 'to put the topstone to this work and make the nation happy' [1, iii, *pp. 434–43*]. MPs, in contrast, regarded themselves as members of a constituent assembly which must amend and perhaps replace the Instrument of Government. No recognised procedure existed for reviewing the Instrument; nor did Cromwell or his Council accept that revision was needed. Most of the parliament's activity consisted of taking the Instrument apart. The Commonwealthmen, who intended to substitute a sovereign parliament, could not be isolated and quickly defeated, partly because they were masters of procedure, but more importantly because much in the hastily compiled constitution did indeed require changing. The Commonwealthmen dexterously played on feelings widespread in the House, such as the desires to safeguard parliament's independence of and control over the executive, to cut taxes and the army's size, and to outlaw religious licence, and as a result frequently carried their motions.

At first Cromwell absolutely denied the MPs' right to question the form of government as established in a single person and parliament. Contending that such debates contravened their election returns, he insisted that all MPs formally acknowledge the permanence of the present form of rule. A large majority, after heart-searching and persuasion, took the required recognition; but between seventy and ninety MPs refused [156]. Those who compromised did so because they could then continue to work in parliament to diminish the Protector's, and greatly augment parliament's, share of the existing authority [*Doc. 7*]. Cromwell, finding that the recognition had not inhibited critics, curtailed debate by specifying four fundamentals contained within the Instrument which must not be altered. The form of government, divided between Protector and parliament, was inviolable. He also stipulated that parliament must never again be able to perpetuate itself, as the Long Parliament had; that control of the armed forces should be shared between the Protector and parliament; and that religious liberty must be preserved.

Discussion was to be confined to circumstantial matters. There were plenty of these to generate heated debate, but MPs would stray back to the forbidden topics. MPs, eager to tighten their control over the executive, decreed that in future all councillors of state must be confirmed in their posts within forty days of parliament's opening. They reviewed the ordinances which Cromwell had already introduced, and suspended his Chancery ordinance while they prepared their own substitute. Then the instinctive conservatism of the majority led them to replace the new county franchise with the old forty-shilling freeholder qualification. The suggestion that £200 property-owners and copyholders should also be enfranchised was defeated. Although the changed voting arrangements had apparently produced a parliament independent of the executive's influence in 1654, MPs wanted to reinstate the familiar system.

The decision to allow parliament to amend the Instrument, if Cromwell was permitted to vet these amendments, showed that some people had worked behind the scenes to prevent the parliament quickly breaking up in disorder. The identity of these pragmatists can only be guessed. Some were probably lawyers anxious that the country should have a workable constitution. Others, like Sir Richard Onslow and Broghill, were prepared to use the Instrument as a starting-point for a better settlement. Those who laboured to reconcile the divergent views of the Protector and MPs probably did so without any active help from Cromwell.

The Commonwealthmen failed to carry proposals that parliament should enjoy sole authority. The majority accepted that to pull down the government in being would be to risk a return to nakedly military rule or a new civil war. But even in this constructive atmosphere, provocative resolutions were passed on the ordering of the armed forces, on the revenues allowed to the Protector, and on the Church. A committee proposed to reduce the standing army, presently directed by Cromwell. The Protector demurred. The House then tried to reduce the army by lessening the amount of the assessment collected each month and by reducing the government's total revenue well below the £2,000,000 required annually. These suggestions, coupled with temporary refusals to sanction the levying of the assessment, deeply disturbed Cromwell. He knew of old that the fastest way to turn the army against parliament was to deny it pay. He also feared that parliament's action would leave the country defenceless at a time of rising danger [*Doc. 8*].

Cromwell was also distressed by the evident intolerance of many MPs. They alleged that his ordinance for triers and ejectors was unsatisfactory. They then challenged his right to veto any laws which infringed religious liberty by arrogating to themselves the exclusive power to enumerate the damnable heresies which should be excluded from toleration. As petitioners from London clamoured for stricter controls, and as MPs silenced the preacher Biddle who had questioned Christ's divinity and the existence of the Holy Spirit, Cromwell discerned how much less tolerant than himself was the majority, inside and outside parliament [195].

Efforts to revise the Instrument constructively foundered on Cromwell's apparent indifference, the volatile behaviour of many MPs and the obstinacy of the Commonwealthmen. By December

1654 some contemplated the reintroduction of monarchy, headed now by King Oliver. Such a course had already been suggested by lawyers and survivors from Pym's old middle group during the later stages of the Rump. It was resurrected by Ashley Cooper, only to be defeated decisively in parliament. Ashley Cooper, disheartened, withdrew from the Council of State and from working on behalf of the Protectorate. By the new year it was clear that the Commonwealthmen, by playing on country animosity towards the army and high taxes, could undo much that their opponents had painstakingly achieved.

Cromwell had no further use for the parliament. Government, at once firm and reforming, was wanted, and he believed that he as Protector could best provide it. The parliament had, under the terms of the Instrument of Government, to sit for five months. Cromwell, to the fury of his critics, calculated this as five lunar months, and on the earliest possible occasion, 22 January 1655, he dissolved the first Protectorate Parliament. The assembly, so far from hastening, had retarded settlement.

PLOTS AND ROYALIST INSURRECTION

The first Protectorate Parliament revealed that much of the electorate and many MPs were still attached to corrupt interests. As soldiers also intrigued and royalists conspired, Cromwell despaired of conciliation and reverted to sharper measures. Commonwealthmen, royalists and the surviving Levellers all hoped to utilise the new unrest in the army. In Ireland Ludlow's public defiance continued to unsettle the soldiery and administration. In Scotland a plot to overthrow the Protectorate was uncovered. Three colonels petitioned Cromwell to abandon the unwholesome experiment of the Protectorate and to return to 'the good old cause' for which they had campaigned together in the 1640s. Cromwell, well informed about these intrigues, thanks to an excellent intelligence service run by his secretary John Thurloe, easily stopped trouble.

Less easily controlled were attacks on the legal basis of the régime in the law courts. This tactic, used by the king's critics in the 1620s and 1630s, was revived when a London merchant, Cony, refused to pay customs duties on the grounds that the present government had no right to them. In the earlier *causes célèbres,* such as Hampden's Case, the royal government had happily let the judges adjudicate, rightly confident that they would find for the king. The Protector lacked this confidence and, rather than let the case come to court, intimidated Cony and his laywers until eventually they backed down. The administration had avoided a rebuff, but had shown a worrying lack of confidence in the legality of its own operations based as they were on the shaky foundation of the Instrument of Government [45, 58, 89].

Cromwell dreaded the separate strands of opposition being knitted into a concerted attack. Yet his hold over the soldiers scarcely faltered, and there were few signs that the aggrieved Common-wealthmen would unite either with the radical sectaries, the Levellers or the cashiered officers. Royalists rejoiced at Cromwell's difficulties, but their hopes of profiting from them were far-fetched. Even so it was the royalists who worried Cromwell most. Since becoming Protector, he had tried to end past divisions, and had encouraged former royalists to re-enter public life. Most of those whose estates had been sequestrated in the 1640s were now allowed to recover them on payment of fines. Cromwell expected this generosity to be repaid with peaceful behaviour. Instead a minority of royalists acted 'as if they meant to entail their quarrel and prevent the means to reconcile posterity'. They persisted in their devotion to Charles II, and educated their children in the same loyalties [117].

Cromwell exaggerated the extent of royalism. He was, however, right to fear the fanaticism of a small group and the unpredictable effects of a new royalist rising on the uncommitted in England. Those who actively schemed for Charles II's return were few in comparison with those who had fought for his father. Most cavaliers wished only to regain and restock their estates. Over 3,000 leading royalists had had to pay fines to recover their patrimonies. These fines, although a burden after the privations of the civil wars, seldom amounted to more than twice the estate's annual yield and were no worse than finding a marriage portion for an extra daughter. Even among the group of 780 obdurate royalists whose estates had been sold by the state, most quickly repurchased their manors [35, 160, 166]. Former royalists might be contemptuous of the usurper, but few were prepared to incur fresh penalities by dabbling in treason. Further-more, Charles II was little known in England, and what was known was not admired. He was reputed to be willing to trade familiar English institutions for continental and Catholic help. His advisers constantly bickered, often for personal ascendancy, but also to dictate policy. The cautious, like Edward Hyde, contended that 'it must be the resurrection of the English courage and loyalty must recover England to the King', and denounced any deal with Presbyterians and Catholics as likely to estrange the king's natural supporters, committed to episcopacy, in England. They were opposed by the headstrong and the flexible, who included the king's Catholic mother, Henrietta Maria, Sir John Berkeley, Sir Edward Herbert and Lord Jermyn. The dissensions among the exiles were reproduced within the royalist camp in England [11, 117].

Men of substance generally counselled caution. They argued that with time the Protectorate would fall apart of its own accord. Plotting, in any case, tended to be localised and poorly co-ordinated, beset with the same rivalries and sense of local loyalty which had bedevilled royalism in the 1640s. Nevertheless, risings in scattered parts of England were planned for 1655. The cautious, grouped in 'The Sealed Knot', dissociated themselves from these risky designs. Leadership passed to younger sons and ruined squires, unencumbered by the cares of property or family and egged on by zealous episcopalian chaplains. The young king had a choice, either to order his followers to abandon the scheme or all of them to throw themselves wholeheartedly into the fray. Charles, torn between contradictory advice, did neither. The projected risings went off feebly. Only in Salisbury, on 12 March 1655, did much happen. About 200 men, commanded by Sir Joseph Wagstaff, an experienced royalist soldier recently returned from the continent, and John Penruddock, a local man, broke open the jail. Few joined the rebels, who, having been chased into Devonshire, were defeated within two days [128].

This sorry affair cautioned royalists against further insurrections. Yet it also cautioned Cromwell. The rebels had been defeated easily, and were soon punished by the local courts. At first Cromwell minimised the episode, describing the insurgents as a 'company of mean fellows, not a lord, nor a gentleman, nor a man of fortune, nor this, nor that, amongst them' [1, iv, *p. 265*]. However the comprehensive and repressive measures which he took in the aftermath of the rising suggested that he detected both a present military danger and a more ominous problem of continuing disaffection. Penruddock's rising was the tip of an enormous iceberg of actual and potential discontent. The escapade also confirmed what the 1654 parliament had already indicated, that he had been wrong to relax and conciliate old enemies.

6 THE SECOND PHASE OF GODLY RULE: THE MAJOR-GENERALS 1655–1656

THE INSTITUTION OF THE MAJOR-GENERALS

The government, apprised of royalist plans, had reinforced the garrisons in London and the ports. In February 1655 the regular troops in London had been supplemented by a militia controlled by new commissioners. In March Cromwell commissioned his brother-in-law, John Desborough, as major-general in the west to suppress Penruddock. Desborough's success suggested that similar means could pacify the entire country. By the summer of 1655 England and Wales had been divided into eleven districts, each supervised by a major-general. So began a phase of Cromwell's rule which is usually interpreted as a wild aberration from his sensible, conciliatory policies, and a relapse into undisguised military dictatorship. Few, at the time or since, questioned the unpopularity of the major-generals or Cromwell's political error in instituting them. Cromwell intended the major-generals to quell disorder and also to solve the problem which had beset him since 1653, how to create a people loyal to his régime. Chastened by the apparent failure of conciliation, he returned in 1655 to the policy, tried briefly in 1653, of allying with the godly and hastening the rule of the Saints in England, and used the major-generals as his local agents in the work [7, 56, 180].

The major-generals were experienced soldiers. Some, like Fleetwood (recently returned from governing Ireland) and Lambert, were required to attend the Council of State in London, and so delegated their work to deputies. Others neglected their duties. The size of the regions they were to oversee varied greatly. Fleetwood and his deputy commanded an area which stretched from Oxfordshire to Norfolk and Essex. James Berry was expected to police much of the Welsh Border and mid and north Wales.

The major-generals' first tasks were military: to round up trouble-makers and expel royalist activists. They would be helped by newly recruited militias, paid by a punitive tax, the decimation, collected from those who had necessitated these measures, the royalists. The militia, the traditional defence of each county, had been in the process of revival since 1650. Now special militia commissioners assisted the major-generals in raising, paying and deploying these augmented forces. This part of the system provoked few open protests. Those chosen as militia commissioners varied from county to county. In some shires only soldiers or upstarts would serve; in others, like Cornwall and Somerset, local gentlemen were prepared to accept the office [42, 55, 83, 118]. More unpopular was the decimation tax. Those who had plotted the overthrow of the Protectorate would either be imprisoned or exiled, and would forfeit two-thirds of the profits of their property to the state. Known adherents of Charles II, even if they had not rebelled lately, would also be jailed or banished. However, the main cost of the new militia would fall on a much larger group, identified not by their present behaviour or philosophy, but by their past actions. Those who had fought against the Long Parliament or had had their estates sequestrated for political dis-affection in the 1640s were subjected to a tax of 10 per cent if they owned land worth more than £100 annually, or of £10 annually if they possessed real property valued at £1,500. This scheme was inept. The numbers affected by the tax were small; so few that they could not finance the militia [7]. Those taxed were politically powerful – the very men whom Cromwell must win over and involve in local affairs if his régime was to survive. Many unaffected by the deci-mation tax objected that it contravened the 1652 Act of Oblivion, and kept alive divisions better blurred. By treating placid royalists as disloyal on no solid evidence, the tax might nudge them into revolt. Cromwell answered that the Act of Oblivion had been conditional on the former royalists supporting the régime, and this, he averred, they had failed to do.

These measures were intended both to remove the leaders of any future insurrection and to reduce the number of potential followers. Cromwell was alarmed by the dissolute and masterless men who travelled the country and congregated in the towns. Their numbers had grown since the Civil War and they seemed willing to be subverted by the royalists. Cromwell wanted them disciplined, and asked that those who could not work should be distinguished from those who would not. The former would be relieved by charity; the latter would either be set to work or transported to the colonies. Gatherings of the idle and discontented would be restricted, first by closing isolated alehouses and also by banning horse-races, cock-fights, bear-baitings and plays. The roads were to be cleared of desperadoes. Greater care would be taken to log foreigners entering the country. Furthermore, masters would be expected to supervise their servants' activities and to guarantee their good behaviour. Indeed a comprehensive register of the names and whereabouts of all potential troublemakers was planned, with particular vigilance for London. Inevitably, the control achieved by these means was incomplete.

No seventeenth-century government in England was better informed about likely malefactors. Even so the detailed information did not touch the secret loyalties of the provinces, or shield Cromwell against a dedicated assassin. However, the major-generals possessed other powers intended to change the temper of the populace. Cromwell regarded the stubborn episcopalian clergy who still officiated in country mansions and private chapels as important in the survival of royalism, and determined to silence them. The major-generals should improve the work of the triers and ejectors, and eject all the malignant clergy as the essential prelude to a more thorough assault on ungodliness. For the same reason the re-formation of manners, abated but not suspended in 1654, must be intensified. The major-generals themselves were instructed to set a pattern of godliness and virtue, and to enforce 'the laws against drunkenness, blaspheming and taking the name of God in vain by swearing and cursing, plays and interludes, and profaning the Lord's Day . . . ' [148, 165].

The combination of the major-generals' strong military character and their programme of banning 'cakes and ale' might be expected to make them uniquely unpopular. Yet, at least for a time, they were obeyed and even helped by some of the substantial gentry. As agents of the central government the major-generals were inevitably disliked, as earlier royal commissioners and nominees had been. The fact that they continued the military government of the 1640s and now served a usurper added to the animosity. But the major-generals also possessed power, to favour and help, to relax in particular cases the severity of ordinances, to relay local concerns to London, and to bestow prestigious local offices. Some provincial notables cultivated those who presently wielded power over them, and thereby pleasantly surprised the major-generals [*Docs 10 and 11*].

Another reason why the major-generals were helped was the support among a well-organised minority for the godly reformation which was now to be speeded. Cromwell had been taxed with retreating from this cause after the end of the Barebones Parliament, but he vigorously denied it. Cromwell's difficulty, which led to much misunderstanding among contemporaries, was his wish to revive familiar institutions, notably the commission of the peace in the counties and the borough magistracy, and at the same time to achieve radical reforms. The major-generals were seen as a means of reconciling these two apparently divergent objectives. By adding the major-generals to the commissions of the peace in their districts, and by nominating godly magistrates to assist them, the traditional organ of local government would be strengthened and turned into an instrument of godly rule [*Doc. 10*]. Indeed the major-generals became the latest device to cure the endemic inefficiency of local government [56, 165].

Since at least Elizabeth's reign the haphazard operations of the JPs had periodically been augmented by special commissioners, charged with particular tasks and better supervised by the Privy Council. Most of these initiatives were unavailing. The central government lacked the money to create a more malleable local bureaucracy to replace the JPs, and in any case realised that appointment as a magistrate was a cheap way to sweeten men of consequence. Only in the 1640s, under the imperatives of warfare, had many of the JPs' powers been transferred to agents of the Long Parliament. Those who normally might have expected to govern their shires as magistrates resented their own loss of power, especially to men of inferior breeding and limited wealth.

In the wake of the civil wars the revolutionary régime had to win over men of influence in the counties if it was to survive. One means of reconciling such men was to revive the commission of the peace and to nominate them to it. Such a policy was followed, rather erratically, in the 1650s. The trouble was that Cromwell regarded local government both as an arena where members of the leading county dynasties could become involved with the régime, and as a method of consolidating the revolution by pressing on with reform. Some former royalists and moderates, and their uncommitted sons, did serve the Protector as magistrates. But the majority of active justices were newcomers – parochial gentlemen, tradesmen and fervent Calvinists – who used their authority to fashion godly commonwealths in their localities. Because their time and resources were limited, the justices tended to select from the multiplicity of laws and ordinances those which best suited their needs or temperament, and thereby diverged from the programme planned by Cromwell and his Council of State. Cromwell lampooned the negligent justices. Matters would, however, be improved by the major-generals who would point the magistrates to the laws most in need of enforcement and would back those justices already attending to such matters. Cromwell expected much – too much – from the eleven major-generals: that they would simultaneously overawe opposition, revitalise local government and hasten the rule of the Saints in England.

THE MAJOR-GENERALS AT WORK

Cromwell believed that the major-generals' successes outweighed their failures. He publicly praised them for having been 'more effectual towards the discountenancing of vice and settling religion than anything done these fifty years', and declared that he would retain the system 'notwithstanding the slander of foolish men'. The major-generals easily performed their military tasks, owing to the disarray of their opponents and the dejection of the royalists. But finance soon gave trouble. The decimation tax, unpopular in itself, failed to pay the costs of the new militia. The yield stayed low because the Protector and the local commissioners exempted some liable to the tax, and because the prudent Cromwell refused to lower the threshold at which the tax was paid. By the summer of 1656 the financing of the system had been centralised, and was supplemented from other revenues. Because the budget was in serious deficit, since credit had almost dried up and as costs had been much increased by war against Spain, it was obvious that change must come [7, 37, 180].

The major-generals had difficulty in assessing accurately their impact on local affairs. They often magnified the exceptional and unusual instances of support in order to convince the Protector that they were doing their work well [*Doc. 10*]. Some, like Kelsey in Kent and Goffe in Sussex, were hampered by their lack of local connections and knowledge [50, 55]. Others were too well-known, so that their humble origins were derided. The system depended too much on the activity and commitment of each major-general to accomplish comprehensive improvements. In turn, the major-generals were at the mercy of the local notables and those who came forward to assist, and of the uneven help offered by the central government.

Major-General Worsley, overseer of Lancashire, Cheshire and Staffordshire, was unusual in his zeal: he closed unlicensed alehouses and silenced malignant clergy. Yet many of his activities fitted into a pattern already well established in north-west England. The proliferation of alehouses, which consumed scarce foodstuffs, spawned idleness, intrigue and immorality, and invited down the anger of God, had pained the godly for decades. At times of dearth in the past JPs had shut many alehouses in response to popular pressure. But when the crises had passed, taverns soon sprang up again. In the later 1640s, when many of the poor starved, fresh efforts had been made to reduce the number of alehouses. Worsley, to the approval of sober and godly men, resumed and intensified those earlier campaigns. He also sought to improve poor relief, to provide work and to control the prices and distribution of vital commodities. These were all matters which magistrates were supposed to look to, and which had been attended to from time to time. Worsley simply endorsed and strengthened local efforts, which of late had become more effective when committees of godly and responsible men in many Cheshire villages had regulated community affairs [83].

Perhaps Worsley was unique in the range of his work and in the local aid he received. Exhausted by his exertions, he died prematurely at the age of thirty-four. Most other major-generals reactivated at least some of the social and economic laws which had long been on the statute book but had been laxly observed. In doing so they delighted the godly, who as magistrates had tried to do the same, or who in their congregations had prayed for such rulers. Thus scandalous ministers were rooted out and replaced by diligent preachers. Vagrants were prevented from entering strange districts and burdening the rates. The poor were helped, hospitals sheltered the aged and infirm, wages and prices were fixed, and markets were regulated to stop cheating over weights and measures [67, 69, 104, 137]. But the impact of the major-generals is often impossible to separate from the sustained efforts throughout the 1650s of godly and attentive magistrates, such as Robert Beake in Coventry. Here the level of effective concern during the Interregnum surpassed what had been achieved in the last drive at greater administrative efficiency in the provinces in the 1630s. Elsewhere, the late 1640s and even the 1660s marked the peaks of magisterial activity [56, 69, 103].

In some places godly congregations welcomed the major-generals and urged quicker progress towards the new Jerusalem [*Doc. 12*]. Too close an alliance with this godly party exposed Cromwell and the major-generals to the dangers of relying on a minority, albeit dedicated and well-organised, but hated by the lax majority. Although Cromwell believed that in time godly reformation would improve the temper of that majority, he knew that the change would be slow, and in the interval he had to contain and check popular disaffection lest it weaken his régime.

By the summer of 1656 fresh duties were loaded onto the major-generals. After much dalliance Cromwell concluded a pact with

France. It was aimed against Spain, with whom England was already fighting in the Caribbean: the year of 1656 saw England engaged in a costly war which obliged Cromwell to turn to parliament to supply cash. Like the Stuarts before him, Cromwell expected a patriotic sense of national danger to induce MPs to forget their grievances and to vote generous taxes. The major-generals were instructed to supervise the elections and, where possible, to procure the return of well-affected members.

The major-generals had to contend with electoral arrangements which, by increasing county representation, had been designed to curtail the executive's influence over elections. They were hampered by their own unpopularity, expressed in the slogan 'no swordsmen, nor decimators'. Only in the boroughs, always more easily swayed with their smaller electorates and recently remodelled to make their officers more reliable, did the major-generals have modest successes. The reports reaching Cromwell indicated that many known critics of the Protectorate, headed by Commonwealthmen like Haselrig, would be in the new parliament. Cromwell, urgently needing money from parliament to fight the war and now more experienced in the wiles of the Commonwealthmen, approached his second parliament in a sombre mood [44, 86, 194].

7 THE SECOND PHASE OF HEALING AND SETTLING: THE LORD PROTECTOR 1656–1658

THE END OF THE MAJOR-GENERALS

Cromwell grumbled that the major-generals had persuaded him to call another parliament, confident that they could control both its membership and its debates. As the parliament, scheduled to open on 17 September 1656, approached, he warned leading Commonwealthmen that he would quell their opposition and continue the new system. Certainly opposition could be expected from the large group of the Protector's critics which had been returned [74, 176, 177]. As in 1654 experienced politicians, particularly the Commonwealthmen, had played on the widespread dislike of military dictatorship, innovation and centralisation, continuing high taxes and irksome drives for moral purity. The Protector, on the major-generals' advice, used the powers which had been granted him in the Instrument of Government and excluded almost one hundred of those elected as being improperly qualified. Another forty to sixty MPs, affronted by this act, voluntarily absented themselves. This sweeping purge could not, alas, make a compliant parliament. Too many of the members were newcomers whose opinions were unknown to the government for it to be possible to exclude all potential critics. The majority of MPs were again drawn from the country gentry, and had the preoccupations of their kind.

One obsession soon appeared, distracting members and antagonising Cromwell. The long-standing mistrust of religious liberty had recently been increased by the behaviour of James Nayler. The Quakers,* a new sect, alarmed alike by their rapid growth and rejection of theological verities. Like the Ranters, the Quakers were guided by the light within. They rejected the necessity of an ordained ministry or of parish churches, and refused to pay tithes. They denied the usual distinctions of human society. The propertied protested that 'the whole world is governed by superiority and distance in relations, and when that's taken away, unavoidably anarchy is ushered in', and alleged that the Quakers aimed to 'overturn all laws and government' [100]. Nayler was not typical of the generality of Quakers, but his offences made MPs consider both his specific case and the wider problem of the sect. Cromwell too was shocked by Nayler who had ridden into Bristol on a mule, fêted by adoring women, apparently parodying Christ's entry into Jerusalem. Nor did he agree with Quakers' distinctive tenets or believe that heresy should be permitted. However, he was satisfied that the means existed to restrain these excesses, and wished only to stop those acts which might endanger public order [195].

The majority of MPs insisted that the penalties presently available under the Rump's Blasphemy Act were too mild, and wanted to end the liberty which had allowed such views as Nayler's to arise. MPs discussed increasing retrospectively the penalties under the Blasphemy Act or passing an Act of Attainder against Nayler. Either course might invite Cromwell's intervention, since the Instrument entrusted him with the defence of religious freedom. Ingenious MPs explored ways to circumvent Cromwell and proposed to annex to parliament the judicial powers of the now defunct House of Lords and to act as a court. Cromwell disliked parliament's high-handed action, which culminated in Nayler being pilloried, branded, whipped, having his tongue bored and being imprisoned. He was yet more annoyed at the skill with which MPs had evaded his power to maintain religious liberty. Nayler's case showed that an intolerant parliament could be tempted to act rashly. Cromwell began to appreciate the value of a second chamber (which he had never wanted abolished), to check the Lower House and to exercise legally the judicial powers of the old House of Lords [*Doc. 15*].

Deciding how to punish Nayler distracted MPs from their chief task, voting supply. A first step was to continue, and perhaps extend, the decimation tax. On Christmas Day 1656 Major-General Desborough introduced a Bill to renew the tax [*Doc. 13*]. This was the one issue calculated to unite civilian MPs against the government. MPs vyed with each other to condemn the decimation, both for contravening the Act of Oblivion and for rekindling old animosities. They also attacked the major-generals paid by the tax as military tyrants. The major-generals vainly defended the levy on grounds of the growing royalist menace. Lambert depicted the royalists, while the debate went on, as 'now merry over their Christmas pies, drinking the King of Scots's health, or your confusion'. The country gentry, given the chance, buried the major-generals. On 20 January 1657 the Bill to continue the decimation tax was rejected by 124 votes to 88. For an instant the country, at war, teetered on the brink of chaos. However the MPs, eager to show that they were not wreckers, soon came forward with an alternative to the major-generals. Also, as an earnest of good will to the Protector parliament voted £400,000 towards the war.

KINGSHIP

On 23 February 1657 a remonstrance was presented to parliament, in which Cromwell was asked to assume the title of king. At the end of March, after detailed debates, a new constitution, the Humble Petition and Advice, was offered to Cromwell. The proposals would transform the precarious elective Protectorate into a hereditary Cromwellian monarchy [*Doc. 14*]. Moreover, they would rest on the authority of parliament and not, as with the Instrument of Government, on an unrepresentative caucus of soldiers.

Political instability since 1649 had increased the appeal of monarchy. Cromwell himself had been reluctant to see monarchy abolished. By 1652 his former parliamentary allies, notably St John and the lawyer Whitelocke, were arguing that only a monarchical settlement could stabilise the country. Others, including Lambert in 1653 and Ashley Cooper in 1654, reached the same conclusion. Recent events had convinced more country gentlemen and lawyers of the importance of the régime shedding its strong military carapace. The Protector's worsening health and the repeated plots to kill him meant that his death and the succession must be faced. Recent policies in Scotland and Ireland had also shown how the régime's dependence on the soldiery could be lessened and how instead the Protectorate could win over men of local importance [114, 135, 150].

While the major-generals had ruled England, Henry Cromwell in Ireland and Lord Broghill in Scotland had divested the Protectorate of some of its unpopular features. Each had judged that neither country would be secure while it was governed by the sword, and set out to construct an alliance with some of the influential indigenous inhabitants. By tempering his father's policies and deferring, perhaps too much, to local interests, Henry Cromwell won over a section of the Protestant landowners settled in the island before 1641. In Scotland Broghill, temporarily president of the Council there, reconciled some of the Presbyterian clergy and educated laity. In both countries English rule still rested on a very narrow base. Henry Cromwell's and Broghill's constructive and conciliatory policies could easily be reversed by the London government. In order to safeguard what they had already achieved, and also to extend their experiments, they asked that similar policies be introduced into England. As a consquence Broghill promoted, and Henry Cromwell backed, the Humble Petition and Advice, because the settlement would base government 'upon persons of estate, interest, integrity and wisdom' [135, 150].

The supporters of kingship, apart from a useful contingent of Irish and Scottish MPs marshalled by Broghill, included country squires such as Sir Richard Onslow and Sir Charles Wolseley, and the lawyers Whitelocke and John Glynn. They played successfully on the conservative instincts of the unpolitical majority, wearied by constant experiments. Ranged against them in parliament were the major-generals and their clients. At once it was discerned that the controversy would centre on the title of king. Rather than put that question to the test at once, it was postponed until the other parts of the constitution were agreed [*Doc. 14*].

Another obvious novelty was the proposal to reintroduce a second chamber into parliament. Otherwise the Humble Petition and Advice improved on those features of the Instrument found wanting. Two matters which had of late exercised MPs were now settled to their satisfaction. The qualifications of newly elected MPs would no longer be vetted by Cromwell and his councillors, but by a special panel of commissioners. Over taxation, it was stated that parliament's consent would be needed for every tax. Cromwell's régime was assigned an annual income of £1,300,000 to be raised in the main from the customs, excise and assessment. It was specified that no money should come from a land tax, at once scotching any thoughts of reviving or extending the decimation.

In its other aspects the constitution was a new version of the old tripartite system of King, Lords and Commons, modified in the ways earlier proposed by Pym. Cromwell as king would be advised by a powerful Council of State, over whose choice and dismissal Parliament would have some control. Parliament's consent would be necessary for appointments to the great offices of state and, after Cromwell's death, for those to military commands. Parliament, though still a junior and irregular partner in government, gained greater weight; triennial meetings were safeguarded. Its membership would be less influenced by the executive now that a team of adjudicators was to test qualifications. Its supremacy over taxation was acknowledged, and it would share with the monarch control of the armed forces.

In religious affairs the new scheme deviated little from the framework laid down by the Instrument and actually erected by the Protector. There was fresh hope that a Confession of Faith could be formulated which would then serve as the test of orthodoxy for parochial ministers. But divines, though they had long worked on such a document, still could not agree [92]. Dissenting churches outside the state system would be permitted, but fewer than before. As well as Roman Catholics and Episcopalians, those who denied the Holy Trinity or blasphemed, profaned or disturbed the peace, were denied liberty to worship. Some sectaries objected to this newly narrowed toleration, which Cromwell apparently approved. Some religious Independents who had hitherto regarded Cromwell as their patron actively opposed the whole Humble Petition and Advice.

At first the scheme had been violently attacked by the leading generals, Lambert, Desborough and Fleetwood. The fixity of their opposition quickly weakened. Cromwell himself warned the officers in London that he was tired of being their drudge and regretted following some of their recent advice. He approved the constructive spirit among MPs and was delighted at last to have a parliament willing to co-operate with him [*Doc. 15*]. Within his own council kingship was supported by Henry Lawrence, Philip Jones (the ruler of South Wales), Edward Montagu who commanded the navy, Charles Wolseley, Secretary Thurloe and Nathaniel Fiennes, Cromwell's former associate in the old parliamentary middle group. Some major-generals moderated their hostility when they realised that their own overthrow was final and that opinion was running strongly for kingship. Among the high command only Lambert seemed implacable. Yet even he abandoned his criticism in parliament. Many of the clauses of the Humble Petition and Advice were agreed without trouble and only when the title itself had to be approved did its opponents rally. On 24 March they were easily outvoted, by 123 to 62 votes [*Doc. 14*].

Opponents of the settlement had decided not to prolong the futile struggle in parliament, but instead to work where their chances of success were greater. Lambert organised the army in the environs of London for political action. Since 1649 the forces had been re-modelled and their attitudes were incalculable. Some criticised Lambert's motives in attacking the settlement when he had proposed something similar in 1653, and accused him of personal ambition. Undoubtedly if the succession to Cromwell was disputed, as was likely under the Instrument, the army would interpose decisively, and probably on Lambert's behalf. Yet Lambert genuinely feared the effects of Cromwell's new alliance with the constitutional monarchists, and suspected that once it had been made Cromwell would desert the cause of reform which he and the army had promoted throughout the last decade [190].

The old radical network, of Leveller penmen, aggrieved officers and political parsons, busied itself to frustrate the Humble Petition and Advice. Cromwell, subjected to clamant advice and torn by his own conflicting impulses, retired into solitary reflection. He was reluctant to abandon the colleagues in the army and the sects with whom he had shared so many aims and experiences. Yet he knew if the country was to be secure, government must rest on a broader foundation than soldiers and a godly élite. He had always wanted to involve the old governing classes in politics once more, and the new settlement seemed the way to do so. He shared the traditionalists' affection for the name of monarchy. But against this had to be set his conviction, which had made him accept the disappearance of monarchy from England, that God 'hath blasted the title', and that he should not defy God and 'seek to set up that which Providence hath destroyed and laid in the dust . . . ' [1, iv, *p. 473*].

Petitions inflamed Cromwell's doubts, while MPs reasoned with him [*Doc. 16*]. Cromwell said 'No' once, at the start of April 1657 [*Doc. 14*]; but the sponsors of kingship persisted. Cromwell spelt out the precise points which he disliked, and the scheme was amended. In particular the annual allocation of money was raised to £1,900,000. Old comrades counterattacked. One reminded how the veteran soldiers opposed the plan, and warned 'those that are for a crown, I fear you have little experience of them'. By May 1657 most observers predicted that Cromwell would accept the Humble Petition and Advice [150]. Lambert, Fleetwood and Desborough threatened that if he did so they would surrender their military commissions. They may also have inspired junior officers to petition against the settlement. On 8 May a petition, organised by Colonel Pride and drafted by Dr Owen, Cromwell's former chaplain and his nominee as vice-chancellor at Oxford, was presented to parliament. Later the same day Cromwell announced, 'although I think the government doth consist of very excellent parts, in all but that one thing, the title . . . I am persuaded to return this answer to you, that I cannot undertake this government with the title of King' [1, iv, *pp. 513–14*]. The kingship group, recently so confident, was stunned, and some of its leaders withdrew immediately from Westminster. Others remained to salvage something, and on 25 May persuaded Cromwell to adopt the Petition and Advice in place of the discredited Instrument, but without the title of king [86, 141].

A rational explanation of Cromwell's unexpected refusal would assume that he feared the spread of disaffection through the army and sects. According to such a view, Cromwell calculated that the new support from respectable landowners and merchants would not compensate for the loss of military backing. Yet subsequent events showed that unrest in the army was slight and could easily be contained. Moreover, Cromwell's aim throughout the 1650s seemed to be to rely on substantial civilians, to whom kingship appealed, and to reduce the régime's reliance on the soldiery. In the end Cromwell probably rejected the title for less rational reasons. He was distressed by the allegations that he had worked for his own and his family's aggrandisement, and that in restoring monarchy he would be disobeying God's command. Already, setbacks, notably in the repulse of the Hispaniola expedition, had shaken his confidence that providence still owned all his and his army's actions. Nor was he persuaded by the lawyers' arguments that monarchy was the only system known to the English laws. Disingenuously Cromwell argued that the Instrument of Government, for all its novelty, had been obeyed throughout the nation. This statement ignored the misgivings of some judges and the embarrassment caused by incidents such as Cony's Case. Cromwell tended to dismiss the title of king as inconsequential, 'a gaudy feather in the hat of authority', and to believe he could have all the benefits of the new settlement – the right to choose his successor, a second House and a solid body of provincial supporters – without it. Finally, Cromwell instinctively reverted to his stance in earlier crises: to balance opposed groupings and to avoid rupturing old ties [189, 192].

THE LAST MONTHS OF CROMWELL

Among those who thought that Cromwell had been wrong to refuse the crown was Edward Hyde, one of the most perceptive royalists. Hyde believed that the majority of Englishmen preferred to live under a king, but that their preference was for the institution and not for an individual. Cromwell, the incumbent ruler, surrounded by a formidable, undefeated army, presiding over a government which modestly reformed and championed the Protestant cause, had enormous advantages over Charles Stuart. The chances of the exiled Charles supplanting King Oliver would be small indeed.

Those who favoured kingship were pleased by Cromwell's toughness towards their opponents. Lambert was the first victim. Unwilling to swear the oath now required of councillors of state, he was dismissed. He retired to the royal manor at Wimbledon, where he cultivated wallflowers and tulips. For the moment the laying aside of Lambert, supposedly the soldiers' darling, caused scarcely a stir. However, he was strengthening his contacts with the disaffected in London and the army, and would in time utilise them [127].

A similar determination marked Cromwell's dealings with the second session of parliament, which opened in January 1658. The need for money to continue the Spanish War had obliged Cromwell to reassemble parliament. Although no new elections had been held, the parliament's active membership had changed since 1657. The reason was that the Upper House, established by the Petition and Advice, had to be filled. Former parliamentary friends from the middle group, like Lord Saye and Sele and St John, to whom Cromwell had nervously offered peerages, contemptuously rejected them. Instead the Protector bled the talent from the Lower House. Broghill, Onslow, Whitelocke, Wolseley and Glynn, who had organised the new system, were removed to the Upper Chamber. Inevitably the leadership of the Commons would pass to others, and another change, resulting from the new constitution, determined the identity of those leaders. The right to adjudicate members' credentials had been transferred from the Protector and his council to a special committee. The latter, tendering only a mild oath, allowed in the fierce Commonwealthmen, like Scot and Haselrig, who had been kept out in 1656. The Commonwealthmen took over the Commons, and once more, instead of accepting the constitution and voting the Protector supply, they tried to undo the Humble Petition and Advice. Their oaths had at least inhibited them from questioning the Protector's authority, but they were free to savage the second chamber [53].

Experience of the trials of settling the country had hardened Cromwell against opponents with their familiar, destructive tactics. He also dreaded an invasion while MPs wrangled. In February 1658 the Spaniards, with whom Charles II had allied in a desperate ploy to recover his throne, were briefly able to free troops and vessels for an expedition against England. Cromwell feared that if the parliament continued, it would deny his troops pay and supplies and so leave the country inadequately defended. Another aspect of the situation alarmed him. After years of talk, Cromwell's opponents had at last formed an incongruous popular front against him. In the past Cromwell had correctly supposed that the differing objectives of the disgruntled sectaries, the aggrieved soldiers, the Commonwealthmen, and the few surviving Levellers were too great to allow an effective alliance. By 1658 the aims of these groups had not altered, but they had been pushed into the background by a more urgent wish which all shared: to be rid of Cromwell and his Protectorate. The joint programme of this coalition included the Commonwealthmen's request that government should be exercised by a sovereign, single-chamber parliament. What they wanted was a new Rump. (Their allies in the sects and army had temporarily forgotten how they had hated the Rump.) The sectaries put into the programme a demand for religious freedom, which they felt was endangered by the Humble Petition and Advice. The soldiers asked for greater control over the choice of their officers, some of whom had recently been removed for political unreliability [*Doc. 17*]. Cromwell did not wait to test how strong or durable this ominous alliance was. He cashiered a group of troublesome junior officers, all members of his regiment. Thereby he gave notice that insubordination in the army at a time of national emergency would never be tolerated. He also dissolved parliament [10, 187].

The danger receded. The Spaniards required their men for service in Flanders; the royalists, deprived of military aid, returned to endless recriminations. The Commonwealthmen, without the public platform of parliament, were reduced to imaginative projecting [107, 178, 193]. Grumbling went on, but usually in private. Meanwhile, Cromwell stumbled on. He had yet to ally unequivocally with the constitutional monarchists, and as a result still lacked an extensive enough body of supporters throughout the country to be able to do without military backing. Deeply involved in a foreign war, Cromwell needed domestic peace, and dealt brusquely with those who disrupted it. His ties with old colleagues loosened when they conspired with the Commonwealthmen. He suspected that 'the good old cause', to which he was asked to adhere, had become a slogan behind which many sorts of self-interest sheltered. The weary disillusion of Cromwell encouraged fresh talk of kingship [141].

In the localities Cromwell courted those whom the Humble Petition and Advice had been intended to please. Members of prominent county families, often the sons of cavaliers, were made justices of the peace and assessment commissioners. The success of this policy depended not only on the Protector's willingness to use such men, but also on the nominees' preparedness to serve. Some undoubtedly refused. Although most gentlemen were too cautious to plot against the régime, many still would not take office under it. Historians of different areas have disagreed about how far conciliation had progressed. By 1657 local government in Wales was said to be the most representative since 1642, 'representative not only of the new Wales that had sprung up during the Commonwealth, but also of the pre-war Wales that was being tempted back into political life by the apparent stability of the Protectorate' [48 *p. 161*]. Another historian has modified this picture, by reminding us that not all those approached served, and also by showing that the godly activists who had dominated the magistracy for much of the decade still did most of the work. A similar situation was to be found in Sussex. There local government had been reopened to men with neutral or royalist pasts. A small group of young gentlemen still plotted on behalf of Charles II, but the prevalent feeling among the county élite was of 'widespread but grudging acceptance of the Cromwellian régime' [56 *p. 314*]. The Protector was obeyed because 'any government is better than no government, and any civil better than a military government' [48, 55, 56 *p. 316;* 67, 69, 83, 103, 118].

Cromwell's eagerness to employ such men in the provinces raised hopes that politicians with similar backgrounds might be added to the Council of State. Cromwell, however, preferred to balance his council between the contending factions. He received contradictory advice from his councillors, and responded with his favourite tactic, political opacity. The speculations which abounded in 1658, that a new parliament would be summoned, and that, if it offered him the crown, he would accept, remained without solid basis.

Cromwell's slow, at times almost imperceptible, progress towards reconciliation may have been carefully calculated. Time, rather than forceful acts, might make his rule familiar and acceptable, and erase old allegiances. Foreign entanglements and his own weariness may also have obliged Cromwell to act circumspectly. Uncertain how to read providence, manifest in recent events, he retreated into introspection. Some kept their peace because they sensed that the Cromwellian order was nearing its end. A Quaker who visited the Protector in August 1658 reported: 'I saw and felt a waft of death go forth against him, that he looked like a dying man' [1, iv, *pp. 867–8*). On 3 September 1658, a day of tempests and the anniversary of the victories of Dunbar and Worcester, Oliver Cromwell died.

8 EPILOGUE: TOWARDS THE RESTORATION OF CHARLES II

The events between September 1658 and May 1660, when Charles II returned to London as King, are often treated as a confused epilogue in which all hurried towards the Stuarts' inevitable restoration. Confused these months certainly were. But the inevitability of Charles II's return is more questionable, at least until the beginning of 1660. One theme ran through these hectic days as it had through the preceding decade: the need for a stable and acceptable form of government. None of the systems tried between 1658 and 1660 offered even the imperfect security of the Cromwellian Protectorate [72].

At first the Cromwellian system continued, headed now by the inexperienced civilian, Richard Cromwell. The latter, refreshingly free from his father's inconvenient obsessions and unencumbered by sentimental affinities with the soldiery, was an unpolitical squire, similar in background and outlook to many in the political nation. He might attract those who had hitherto hesitated to back the régime, and might also decisively repudiate the army's influence. His early acts encouraged these hopes, as he favoured the champions of kingship and ignored the aggrieved army commanders. Even the parliament which he summoned in January 1659, though again steered by Commonwealthmen, sectaries and soldiers, proved more tractable than expected. The majority in the House, of provincial gentry, was able to prevent the Commonwealthmen and their allies from toppling the Protectorate. But the opposition worked successfully outside parliament and by May 1659 had brought down the Protectorate. Decisive in Richard Cromwell's fall was the defection of his generals, Lambert, Fleetwood and Desborough. Perhaps his father had been wise not to test the resolve of this triumvirate in 1657 by being crowned king. The Protectorate had changed too little to survive without the active backing of the army. Richard Cromwell retired to a long twilight existence in rural obscurity [99].

The allies, united by little more than hatred of the Cromwellian system, had now to devise a substitute government for the British Isles. The army first restored the Rump, forgetful of how little the Rump had pleased it between 1649 and 1653. Local government was ruthlessly purged of those recently tempted back by Cromwell. Radicals again pressed the government to abolish tithes, to humble the lawyers and rigid divines, and reimpose godly discipline. When the Rump failed to respond, it was swept away by the soldiers. In October 1659 a new military dictatorship, exercised by a Committee of Safety, was imposed. Men of substance were appalled and hankered after monarchy. A Cromwellian monarchy was no longer possible, so it must be Charles who would restore normality to the country.

By December 1659 the Committee of Safety had given way again to the Rump which was pressed to do what it had delayed before 1653: specify the conditions on which a new parliament could be elected. In order to make itself more representative, the Rump readmitted seventy-three of those who had been secluded in 1648. This enlarged Rump authorised the calling of a Convention Parliament, which opened on 25 April 1660. When we recall that the Long Parliament had contained a majority anxious to keep the Stuart monarchy, it was small wonder that a majority in the Convention saw a monarchical restoration as the only way to stop the political confusion. Yet, just as in 1648 most MPs thought that Charles I's powers must be limited, so in 1660 politicians in the Convention wished to keep Charles II to conditions similar to those proposed in 1648. The place of parliament in public affairs and policy-making must be guaranteed. The king's freedom to dispose the armed forces and to choose ministers had to be circumscribed. Nor could the old monopoly of the established episcopalian Church be reimposed without some care for the numerous sects which had burgeoned in its ruins. However, the politicians eager to hold Charles II to terms were defeated by the unpolitical majority in parliament. The latter wanted to end the uncertainty and regain their own local pre-eminence by bringing back the king immediately. The king's advisers, notably Hyde, cleverly created the impression that the king would submit to terms once restored. On 29 May Charles II triumphantly re-entered London, having been kept to no treaty. Once repossessed of his throne, it would cause contention to deprive him of traditional rights. Contention was what everyone wanted to avoid, having experienced too much in the last twenty years, and as a result few limits confined the restored king. Many of the questions disputed between 1640 and 1660, and then dropped abruptly for fear of hindering a settlement, would be resolved only after another revolution, that of 1688–89.

PART THREE: ASSESSMENT

9 THE IMPACT OF THE RÉGIME

Cromwell founded no durable régime. After 1660 Charles II regained most of his father's power. The ordinances and acts of the Interregnum were jettisoned. Accordingly, it would be easy to conclude that the experimentation of the 1650s left little trace in a restored monarchy. Such a judgement would be too facile.

During the 1650s, the state – in Scotland and Ireland as much as in England – obtruded more into ordinary lives. Warfare itself, although sporadic and localised, killed many and left more maimed, widowed, orphaned or impoverished. In England it has been calculated that nearly 85,000 perished [84, 85]. Such mortality, mainly of able-bodied men, may have slowed population growth thereafter. This slackening lessened pressure on land, work and food. Thanks also to plentiful harvests throughout the 1650s conditions for many of the survivors improved. Crops and buildings had been destroyed; horses, oxen and wagons had been commandeered. But such losses were soon made good. Less easily effaced was the impact on individuals' lives, whether through the death or disabling of a partner or parent or the loss of a precious beast or tools [185]. Furthermore, the depredations of armies did not cease in 1649. Soldiers were moved to and fro between England, Ireland and Scotland. Regulars and conscripts were deployed in the Dutch and Spanish wars. Numerous garrisons still dotted the countryside, their occupants often unwelcome. What they spent locally had to be balanced against what they simply took. Then, too, troops assisted tax collectors, shielded Baptists and Quakers, fathered bastards and intimidated civilians. The thousands lately demobbed were only with difficulty assimilated into civilian life.

The numbers in the army dropped: from perhaps 60,000 in 1653, to 53,000 in 1654 and 36,500 by 1659 [189]. Simultaneously the navy expanded. Between 1649 and 1660, two hundred and sixteen ships were added to a fleet of about fifty. At the same time, probably 20,000 mariners were afloat [40]. The numbers of serving soldiers at all levels of civil government remained surprisingly low. Thus, four soldiers among the councillors of state were easily outnumbered by ten civilians. Of nearly 2,500 JPs, only 123 were officers. Yet, the pervasive influence of the military throughout the decade can scarcely be denied. Army commanders, after all, had determined the political initiatives from the king's trial and execution, through the establishment of first Barebones and then the Protectorate, to the eventual fall of Richard Cromwell and the restoration of Charles II. Cromwell's power always rested on his mastery of a colossal army and navy, despite his attempts to enlarge his support elsewhere [44, 189].

Provincials were reminded continuously of the military: not just when posses clattered through their streets or veterans exhibited their wounds, but when, as in Coventry in 1654, householders pleaded to be compensated for what had been destroyed nearly ten years earlier [103]. Above all, the higher taxes which sustained the military machine brought home how militarised the country had become even in comparison with the 1620s when last it had been on a war footing. Unpopular as the levies were, the régime succeeded in collecting the monthly assessment and the excise payable on a long list of commodities. The population, it has been suggested, was habituated during this period to permanently enhanced levels of taxation which could continue and which would make possible the imperial expansion after 1689 [37]. Moreover, the larger apparatus of assessors and tax gatherers drew more into the increasingly uniform operations of the state, even in its remotest regions. Maybe, the obloquy which attached itself to the Cromwellian system arose less from its strongly military hue than from its being a government of high taxation.

Scotland and Ireland were more severely damaged by warfare than most English districts. Ten per cent of adult Scotsmen may have died in the protracted fighting. In Ireland, as much as one-third of the total population was thought to have been lost between 1641 and 1653. More died of the disease and famine which attended the Cromwellian campaigning after 1649 than on the battlefields [136]. Such casualties were only slowly overcome. Even when lands had been restocked and were again cultivated, the trauma could not be forgotten. Ireland and Scotland were returned to English authority thanks to invasion and reconquest. Although the victors extended the benefits of constitutional incorporation, with Scotland and Ireland each sending thirty members to the Westminster parliament, so unequal were the terms of the enforced unions that they bequeathed fierce animosities. In both defeated countries, English rule had to be upheld by large armies of occupation and through chains of garrisons and forts. The verdict on the Scottish arrangements, of 'an alien, oppressive police state', can hardly be gainsaid [39].

Those charged with governing the Scots on Cromwell's behalf, especially Lord Broghill in 1655, searched for an economical alternative. Many of the customary rulers of the Scottish localities, the aristocrats and lairds, when not killed, had been laid aside as politically suspect. They were also stripped of their judicial powers and tenurial privileges. Adequate substitutes within local society were not easily found. By 1649 most effective power devolved on the sixty presbyteries and 900 kirk sessions, and on the 838 Presbyterian clergymen in the kingdom. Unhappy about much done by the English, they differed in how best to respond to the conquerors. Broghill played upon the divisions. At most he secured a respite from open opposition when one group agreed to cease praying publicly for Charles Stuart as the Scots' own covenanted king [39, 49]. Other collaborators, such as lawyers, townsfolk and university teachers, proved too unrepresentative of indigenous opinion to entrench the Cromwellian order in the affections of the Scots. Particularly in the Highlands and Islands, discontent persisted and was checked only by 10,000 soldiers. After 1660, as in England, the dethroned grandees were reinstated with their old powers. This aristocratic reaction was accompanied by strong anti-English feelings which led to the abandonment for a generation of English efforts to dictate to the Scots [39, 136].

English ambitions to remodel Scottish society never matched, either in outline or practice, what Ireland suffered. Outsiders did not take over Scottish estates. The subjugation of Ireland, in contrast, exposed its élites, if Catholic and royalist, to reprisals. The programme which in the past century had followed earlier Irish rebellions, replacing landlords, office-holders and priests with Protestants from England, Wales and Scotland, was intensified. To civilian settlers were added soldiers whose service in Ireland would be paid in lands. Yet Ireland in the 1650s failed to attract the influx of newcomers on which the success of these plans depended. In 1670 about 8,000 owners had their Irish holdings confirmed: a contingent easily surpassed in size by the Protestants already planted there before 1649. The latter snapped up desirable confiscated properties at bargain prices [36, 134, 135]. Charles II, while tempted to assist loyal Irish Catholics, accepted the essence of the Cromwellian redistributions. As a result, the Catholics' share of Irish land fell from nearly 60 per cent of the total in 1641 to no more than 20 per cent. It would require fresh warfare and conquest between 1689 and 1691 to complete a Protestant ascendancy over land, power and office. This then endured for the next century. But its origins and many of its features can be traced to the 1650s [36, 136].

Cromwell, in appealing to the vanquished Irish to rally to him, distinguished between the landowners and priests, whom he regarded as the authors of the 1641 uprising, and the humble whom they had duped [*Doc. 4*]. Retributive schemes to corral the surviving Catholics into the infertile west were eventually abandoned. Instead they lived scattered across the entire island: a potential threat to English authority. Policy towards the Irish exhibited the long-standing contempt towards a smaller neighbour viewed as barbaric as well as inferior. Ireland was accordingly treated with a savagery rare in the conduct of the fighting in England and lowland Scotland [77, 133, 139, 140]. Yet the victorious Cromwellians believed that they could improve Ireland and the Irish by popularising English agriculture, industry, tenures, habits and religion and by applying English law [34]. Plans conceived in London were tested in Ireland, with scant attention to local needs and with mixed results. Under the government of Henry Cromwell after 1655 ambitions contracted. He cultivated the established Protestants [135]. Among the Catholic Irish (probably 80 per cent of the population) more relaxed conditions, improving harvests and trade and the presence of an enormous army obliged them to submit to Cromwellian rule. The civil wars, caused by Charles I's mishandling of his three kingdoms, had embraced England, Scotland and Ireland. The puny republic in order to be secure was obliged to conquer the two outlying territories. The aftermath of these campaigns brought both under tighter English control. Indeed, a *de facto* union of the three states resulted. So, far from integrating Scotland and Ireland better into a British system, the experiences of the 1650s stimulated a tenacious particularism which would later express itself in nationalism and moves for separation [39, 95].

The revolution of 1649 shook but did not permanently alter England's society and economy. In the early 1650s the massive confiscations of crown, Church and royalists' lands offered a chance to create a nation of peasant proprietors. Portions of these assets passed to tenants and soldiers, but most fell to substantial landowners and merchants [84, 89, 159, 160]. Existing patterns of land ownership were modified only slightly and, in most cases, temporarily. In 1660 the King and re-established Church recovered their lands. Even before then, royalists were buying back their manors when sold by the state.

In Lancashire and Yorkshire royalists succeeded in regaining three-quarters of what they had forfeited [35, 166]. Only a minority, already indebted in 1641 or borrowing recklessly to repossess properties, overreached themselves. By the end of the century the cumulative effect of their troubles obliged them to sell. These unfortunates tended to view the civil wars as the watershed at which their ruin began [160]. Rural tenants and townspeople who had looked to the radicals of the 1640s to improve their lots were disillusioned to see the zeal with which the structures and orthodoxies of the past were already being repaired in the 1650s [65, 89, 103].

The unpopularity of an unfamiliar régime, at its worst in Scotland and Ireland, is to be explained in England by more than its costs and military character. Behaviour and opinions were monitored. This vigilance contrasted sharply with the freedom which had prevailed in the disordered years of war. Earnest campaigners for moral rectitude were heartened. In towns from Barnstaple and Dorchester to Lewes, Rye and Coventry, the watchful spied. Not only those who disturbed the peace with drunken antics or ruptured the harmony of their community by cheating over weights, measures and prices or by defaming neighbours, begetting bastards and idling time away, but also the respectable were enmeshed in the supervisory net. In 1644, the familiar May Day jollifications were outlawed. Three years later the traditional festivities at Christmas, Easter and Lent followed. A series of restrictions in 1644, 1650 and 1657 drained Sunday of fun. As an alternative, a new secular holiday on the second Tuesday of every month was invented. The state festival did not supplant the more familiar ones. Equally, moves to simplify baptism (an end to godparents), marriage (no ring and between 1653 and 1657 a civil ceremony) and funerals made traditionalists defend old ways. Ominously for the government, disobedience carried political connotations. Traditional culture could be associated with the Book of Common Prayer (legally banned but still widely used) and the proscribed Stuart monarchy which would uphold such enjoyable rituals [147, 148].

Even where strenuous magistrates, ministers or major-generals targeted drunkards, adulterers, fornicators, vagrants, hoarders and cheats, little lasting improvement has been detected [56; 74]. The Rump, author of severe acts against adultery and swearing, approved the thitherto haphazard drives for moral reform [96; 168]. More miscreants may have been brought to court, but jurors and magistrates were reluctant to convict. Of seven indicted for adultery in Essex during the 1650s, none was hanged. In Middlesex, of twenty-seven charged with the same offence, twenty-five were acquitted; in Devon, twenty-seven of the thirty similarly arraigned were freed [104, 148]. In some counties, the cruel 1640s rather than the easier 1650s called forth the more energetic efforts of magistrates to aid the poor. Studies of local administration during the Interregnum have concluded that the routines were observed, but concur that schemes of moral reformation almost universally failed [56, 165]. These failures depressed the godly: the more so when they were followed so swiftly in 1662 with the reimposition of episcopacy.

During the 1650s zeal for tighter social and moral discipline separated the rigorists from the easy-going. Such divisions were not new. In some measure they underlay the alignments and outcome of the civil wars. In turn, the Cromwellian episode deepened, even perpetuated them. Ideological and sectarian fragmentation thereafter expressed itself in separate churches of Presbyterians, Independents (or Congregationalists), Baptists and Quakers. The scrupulous followed more than 700 ministers of the 1650s who were ousted from their livings in the 1660s. Well into the eighteenth century it has been estimated that 40 per cent of Coventry's inhabitants dissented from the established Church. In addition, the febrile politics of many larger towns, such as Bristol, Chester, Norwich, Taunton and even London itself, owed much to the linkages between religious and political dissent. Those who opposed the later Stuarts' tendencies towards absolutism and priestcraft looked back to the 1650s, if not as halcyon times, then at least as an era when their ideals had been forwarded by those in power. Those nostalgic for the values and views of the Interregnum were necessarily guarded in their utterances. In any case, they craved a powerful parliament and aristocracy rather than a new Cromwell.

The repressive features of a godly dictatorship, added to the heavy taxes and formidable military presence, gave the Cromwellian régime a grim reputation. Yet that very experimentation which in the political sphere spoke of instability, elsewhere had happier implications. Life under the altered order brightened, and not just because of better weather. Those who had hailed the Commonwealth as the culmination of their dreams were soon dejected. Yet some causes for jubilation persisted. The fortunate received jobs, lands and benefits. First the recalcitrant Scots and Irish, next the Dutch, were brought to heel. Ireland, in particular, was opened up more comprehensively to the attentions of English soldiers, investors and careerists. Moreover, the decade pulsated with schemes. Reformers, theoreticians, social engineers, utopians, charlatans and crack-pots deluged the government with ideas. The authorities liked many of the designs to enrich and settle society, but lacked the cash to advance any but the most utilitarian. Even hopes of making education more vocational and technical made little progress. In private, the curious (some of them employees of the state) speculated and experimented. By 1660 the belief that scientific interests were a fitting part of a gentleman's intellectual furniture was strong enough to persuade Charles II to institutionalise this powerful scientific movement by incorporating the Royal Society [123].

The bewildering variety of ideas and attitudes which had thrived in the 1640s abated or was curbed in the 1650s. Censorship now reduced newspapers to two, both sponsored by the state. Nevertheless, the religious pluralism which survived was matched by a plurality of ideas. Literary and artistic diversity flourished. Architectural innovation occurred, again patronised by state functionaries like St John, Attorney-General Edmund Prideaux and Secretary Thurloe [91, 110].

The régime could pride itself on the absence of serious opposition after 1651, at least in England. Plots – and rumours of plots – abounded, but projected uprisings fizzled out. A lucky strike by a lone assassin seemed most likely to plunge the régime into chaos. Even those who stood apart from the Cromwellian order grudgingly admired its standing abroad. Not all welcomed the Dutch and Spanish wars. Measured by prizes and markets won or concessions extorted by treaty, the gains scarcely justified the expenditure of treasure and men. Jamaica, Pula Rum and Dunkirk made a short tally of trophies. Commonwealthmen contrasted the aggression of the Rump with Cromwell's indecisiveness [*Doc. 18*]. At the time, and since, not just the achievements but the aims of these activities have been questioned. Some believe Cromwell's heady talk that he wished to create a Protestant coalition. The Dutch, Swedes and Danes, together with the Protestant cantons of Switzerland and princes of Germany, would unite against Catholic Europe. Others have argued for Cromwell's realism [66, 97, Crabtree in 105, 160]. He protected Britain and Ireland against internal subversives and invaders; he then improved trade. The Dutch War, after early humiliations, went well. Detractors complained that when Cromwell ended it in 1654 he failed to humble the Dutch. However, if Cromwell was interested primarily in preventing Charles Stuart from launching an offensive from Holland, he succeeded. Thereafter treaties were signed with Portugal, Sweden and France. In concert with France, England fought

Spain on land and at sea. The failure to take Hispaniola was offset by the capture of part of the treasure fleet, victory in Flanders and the gain of Dunkirk. In the Baltic, although Cromwell never reconciled the Danes and the Swedes or persuaded the Swedish king to prefer the Protestant cause before that of his dynasty, he stopped any single power from controlling access to the sea. In consequence, Cromwell guaranteed vital naval supplies [182].

These continental successes cost much. Just as the Rump had latterly concentrated on naval warfare to the detriment of domestic affairs, so after 1656 the Protectorate lacked the money both to fight and embark on grandiose social and economic policies. Warfare might benefit those who traded in the Baltic, Mediterranean, West Indies and Portuguese Empire, naval suppliers and military contractors, but the profiteers seldom dug into their own pockets to help the state. Taxes continued to be collected, but with a further loss of political popularity which hastened the high-spending régime towards oblivion. When Cromwell died, the deficit of expenses over income was calculated at £500,000. The soldiers were owed £890,000 [30, 37, 89].

Quickly enough commentators criticised Cromwell's choice of allies. The French connection had not led, as Cromwell had hoped, to the French Protestants being better treated. Instead it enabled France to defeat Spain definitively, and so elevated the France of Louis XIV to a pre-eminence which jeopardised English trade and security [4]. Such consequences could be seen by the mid-1660s; in 1655 it was less easy for Cromwell to foresee the outcome of a struggle which had continued inconclusively for decades. Whatever policy Cromwell chose would be derided in some quarters, and could be expected to damage important branches of trade. More important than the partisans' anger was England's speedy transformation. From pariah of Europe, shunned for killing its anointed sovereign, the republic was wooed as a desirable partner by the great powers. In creating and exploiting this situation England's rulers burnished the state's international lustre.

Just how much the frequent and sometimes momentous changes in London impinged on the country remains hard to assess. Familiar communications, between the royal court, councillors and assize judges and county magnificoes, were interrupted. Others were soon improvised. First the army council, then the Council of State, kept in touch through their agents and acquaintances on the local commissions, in the gathered churches and municipal corporations. Neither the Rump nor the Protectorate disdained propaganda.

Newspapers trod an official line. The visible images of authority changed, from the seals affixed to official documents, coats of arms in public places, flags borne by soldiers and ships, through the maces carried before civic worthies to the coins in purses. Even the illiterate and remote heard what others had from letters and diurnals. Cromwell himself was pictured in engravings and woodcuts as conquering general and supreme magistrate. His prolix speeches were published. Yet, despite the extra gravity which his office as Protector conferred, nothing akin to a cult of Cromwell was promoted in his lifetime [109, 189].

This was in keeping with his own, often voiced disinclination to govern. Back in the 1640s he had been drawn reluctantly into the public arena. He acted for a worried army and the godly apprehensive about repression. Only when conventional authority collapsed did he take on government. He likened his task to that of 'a good constable to keep the peace of the parish' [1, iv, *pp. 470, 729*]. Some who had watched Cromwell's steady ascent, from obscure MP, inspirational commander of cavalry to ruler of England, Scotland and Ireland, doubted his truthfulness when he denied all personal ambition. Commonwealthmen like Ludlow, the lawyer Whitelocke and the Puritan minister Baxter depicted Cromwell's career as a ruthless quest for power [3, 4, 18, 24]. Such interpretations not only demonised Cromwell, but also personalised the 1650s. The events of the decade become inseparable from the biography of Cromwell.

Much that happened in the 1650s, and even more that did not, was independent of any wishes or actions by Cromwell and his entourage. The increasing struggle to wrest a living from sparse resources was eased more by the elements than by any activity of Interregnum administrators. For the bulk of the population, the insistent attentions of tax collectors and garrison inmates were the most likely reminders of the distant usurpers. Once Cromwell had won his wars, he was not one to show himself promiscuously to the populace. When he died, no sermon marked his interment and little grief appeared. Flawed hero he had become even to his close associates. Nevertheless he had personified a régime which, against the odds, he had held together. His death set in train the political confusion out of which a Stuart restoration looks the inevitable outcome.

Cromwell's career baffled contemporaries and has divided later analysts because it lacked consistency. Cromwell was pulled by contrary impulses. He disliked political change and feared social upheaval. At the same time he had shared the life of his soldiers, with the dangers, excitements and frustrations. He accepted that England had been designed by God as the spot where the Saints would reign and give an example to the world. He believed too that liberty of conscience should be preserved. Often he was indecisive. Crucial choices were left to others. He tried schemes and supporters regardless of where they had originated. When occasion demanded he could act authoritatively, as when army discipline faltered, when invasion loomed, when the godly were endangered or when the self-interested feigned godliness. His lack of ambition, both for himself and his sons, was real. In the end, however, after unsuccessful experiments, he was himself obliged to rule and to bequeath power to his elder son. He hoped to preserve or revive familiar institutions. Yet he acquiesced in the abolition of monarchy and baulked at reviving it. An admirer of parliament, he faced a sequence of quarrelsome assemblies, each of which had to be purged or dismissed peremptorily. Those same qualities which so infuriated contemporaries, of procrastination and ambivalence, particularly pronounced as he aged, allowed him to keep his grip on the army and most of its commanders while winning over more civilian conservatives. The merits of this gradualism were proved when Richard Cromwell abandoned it in 1659 and was quickly overthrown.

Cromwell found high office uncongenial, yet discharged it with sober dignity. He wearied himself by attending too closely to the minutiae of government and by trying personally to move opponents from their stances. In his favourite retreat of Hampton Court Palace he consoled himself with the music of the grand organ removed thence from an Oxford college. The world which he confronted in the 1650s had changed from that of the 1620s and 1640s. He, too, had altered, perhaps in ways other than those needed for his new responsibilities. Gone were the exhilaration and camaraderie of the camp. He adjusted awkwardly to the rituals of a court. However, he did not disavow the ideals of his prime. So he presided over a régime which was feared for its military might, which kept the peace and which grappled with the intractable political, social and religious problems of the day. England had been, and would be, worse governed than it was in the 1650s. Nothing in Cromwell's honourable life excused his treatment after 1660 when jubilant royalists exhumed his remains from Westminster Abbey, carried them to Tyburn and there hanged and decapitated his corpse.

PART FOUR: DOCUMENTS

DOCUMENT 1   CROMWELL IN ACTION

Cromwell's aversion from making political decisions was marked. In battle, however, he acted decisively. The nervous energy pent up within him was commented on by two contemporaries when they described his behaviour before the battle of Dunbar in 1650.

(a) [Cromwell] rid all the night before through the several regiments by torchlight, upon a little Scots nag, biting his lips till the blood ran down his chin without his perceiving it, his thoughts being busily employed to be ready for the action now at hand.

Quoted in C. H. Firth, 'The battle of Dunbar', *Transactions of the Royal Historical Society*, new series, xiv (1900), p. 48.

(b) One that I knew and who was present, told me that Oliver was carried as with the divine impulse. He did laugh so excessively as if he had been drunk, and his eyes sparkled with spirits. He obtained on that occasion a great victory, though the action was said to be contrary to human prudence.

Quoted in *Writings and Speeches* [1], II, p. 319.

DOCUMENT 2   **THE SEARCH FOR A SETTLEMENT**

The problem of finding a satisfactory form of government was at the heart of the difficulties of the decade. The lawyer Whitelocke recorded a discussion in the autumn of 1651, in which he, Cromwell, and the former leader of the old middle group, St John, participated. The hankering after monarchy expressed then grew as the decade passed.

Upon the defeat at Worcester, Cromwell desired a meeting with divers members of Parliament and some chief officers of the army at the Speaker's house; and a great many being there, he proposed to them, that now the old King being dead, and his son being defeated, he held it necessary to come to a settlement of the nation: and in order thereunto, he had requested this meeting, that they together might consider and advise what was fit to be done, and to be presented to the Parliament: . . .

Harrison. I think that which my lord general hath propounded is to advise us to a settlement both of our civil and spiritual liberties, and so that the mercies which the Lord hath given in to us may not be cast away: how this may be done is the great question.

Whitelocke. . . . I should humbly offer . . . whether it be not requisite to be understood in what way this settlement is desired, whether of an absolute republic or with any mixture of monarchy.

Cromwell. . . . Whitelocke hath put us upon the right point; and indeed it is my meaning that we should consider whether a republic or a mixed monarchical government will be best to be settled; and if any thing monarchical, then in whom that power shall be placed.

Sir Thomas Widdrington. I think a mixed monarchical government will be most suitable to the laws and people of this nation; and if any monarchical, I suppose we shall hold it most just to place that power in one of the sons of the late King . . .

St John. It will be found that the government of this nation, without something of monarchical power, will be very difficult to be so settled as not to shake the foundation of our laws and the liberties of the people.

Speaker. It will breed a strange confusion to settle a government of this nation without something of monarchy.

Desborough. I beseech you, my Lord, why may not this as well as other nations be governed in the way of a republic.

Whitelocke. The laws of England are so interwoven with the power and practice of monarchy that to settle a government without something of monarchy in it, would make so great an alteration in the proceedings of our law, that you have scarce time to rectify, nor can we well foresee, the inconveniences which will arise thereby.

Colonel Whalley. I do not well understand matters of law, but it seems to me the best way not to have anything of monarchical power in the settlement of our government; and if we should resolve upon any, whom have we to pitch upon? The King's eldest son hath been in arms against us, and the second son likewise is our enemy.

Widdrington. But the late king's third son, the duke of Gloucester, is still among us, and too young to have been in arms against us, or infected with the principles of our enemies.

Whitelocke. There may be a day given for the King's eldest son or for the duke of York his brother, to come in to the Parliament, and upon such terms as shall be thought fit and agreeable both to our civil and spiritual liberties; a settlement may be made with them.

Cromwell. That will be a business of more than ordinary difficulty; but really, I think, if it may be done with safety and preservation of our rights, both as Englishmen and as Christians, that a settlement of somewhat with monarchical power in it would be very effectual.

Much other discourse was by divers gentlemen then . . . generally the soldiers were against anything of monarchy, though every one of them was a monarch in his regiment or company.

The lawyers were generally for a mixed monarchical government; and many were for the duke of Gloucester to be made king; but Cromwell still put off that debate, and came off to some other point; and in conclusion, after a long debate, the company parted without coming to any result at all, only Cromwell discovered by this meeting the inclinations of the persons that spake, for which he fished, and made use of what he then discerned.

Whitelocke [26], III, pp. 372–4.

DOCUMENT 3   A REPUBLICAN PROGRAMME

Convinced Republicans, though few, had plans for structural reforms which should follow the king's execution in 1649, and freely expressed their disappointment with the Rump's timid behaviour. One Republican set out a detailed programme of change, part of which follows.

3. That Providence hath willed us to be a free state and commonwealth, and reason dictates that we should settle ourselves in that government.

4. That there is a vast and inconsistent difference in all the parts of government betwixt a monarchical and a republic.

5. That as essential to monarchy, there must be inequality and dependency of persons and places, throughout the whole land, and all of them to tend to the good of one in chief, and for which there must be forms, councils, laws, terms and actions answerable thereunto.

6. That as essential to a republic . . . there must be equality and independency of persons and places, throughout the whole land, and all of them to the good of all the people in chief, and for which there must be forms, councils, laws and actions answerable thereunto.

7. That hitherto in the change of our government nothing material as yet hath been done, but a taking of the head of monarchy and placing upon the body or trunk of it, the name or title of a Commonwealth, a name applicable to all forms of government, and contained under the former, and as ours stands now very easy, and capable of being returned by a vote into the abolished government . . .

9. That the only way to make this a happy government is not only to abolish all things that were constituted under monarchy, though very good in themselves, yet the best of them have relation and dependency one way or other to it, as may easily be instanced. But to set up a government in all the parts of it suitable to our republic, taking into consideration, the vastness, condition and situation of our land, with the nature and number of the people, and the change of the government, not to be patterned by any Commonwealth ancient or modern . . .

10. That if such a government be not well and speedily accomplished, we cannot assure ourselves from a return to monarchy; if so it must needs prove worse to the people, than it was before, and thereby shall manifest to God and all the world, that we were not worthy of, nor know how in a rational way, to improve God's providence to us, and so deserve that slavery shall betide us, both for our spiritual and earthly wellbeing.

William Hickman to Cromwell, 16 November 1650, printed in [21], pp. 31–2.

DOCUMENT 4   **CROMWELL IN IRELAND**

Cromwell wished to counteract the impression, widespread in Ireland in 1649, that he intended to destroy all its Catholic inhabitants. He insisted that his quarrel was with the leaders of local society, the landowners and priests, and tried, by this declaration and by his reforms, to win the ordinary Irish to the English cause.

For such of the nobility, gentry and commons of Ireland as have not been actors in this rebellion, they shall and may expect the protection in their goods, liberties and lives which the law gives them; and in their husbandry, merchandizing, manufactures and trading whatsoever, the same. They behaving themselves as becomes honest and peaceable men, testifying their good affections, upon all occasions, to the service of the state of England, equal justice shall be done them with the English. They shall bear proportionably with them in taxes. And if the soldiery be insolent upon them, upon complaint and proof, it shall be punished with utmost severity, and they protected equally with Englishmen.

And having said this, and purposing honestly to perform it, if this people shall headily run on after the counsels of their prelates and clergy and other leaders, I hope to be free from the misery and desolation, blood and ruin, that shall befall them, and shall rejoice to exercise utmost severity against them.

A Declaration of the Lord Lieutenant of Ireland for undeceiving of deluded and seduced people, 21 March 1650, printed in [1], II, p. 205.

DOCUMENT 5   **SCOTLAND'S REACTION TO UNION WITH
                ENGLAND**

Scotland's association with the Stuarts exposed it to an English conquest after 1651. The Scots were offered union with the English in the hope that

*the resulting benefits would cure them of their royalist sympathies. As the
following newsletter reveals, few were impressed by this English gesture,
and English authority over Scotland remained precarious.*

On Wednesday last, the Declaration of the Parliament of England for the
union with Scotland, . . . was proclaimed with much solemnity at the market
cross in Edinburgh by beat of drum and sound of trumpet and the cross
adorned with hangings. . . . There was a very great concourse of people at
the proclaiming of it; after the reading whereof the soldiers gave several
shouts, as complying with the Parliament in the free conferring of liberty
upon a conquered people, but so senseless are this generation of their own
goods that scarce a man of them showed any sign of rejoicing. Though the
most flourishing of their Kings would have given the best jewel in their
crowns to have procured a vote in Parliament for their equal shares of
staking in the laws of England.

Newsletter from Leith, 24 April 1652, printed in Firth [12].

DOCUMENT 6   **THE HOPES OF THE GODLY AROUSED**

*Millenarian expectations were excited by Cromwell's decisions to be rid of
the Rump and to summon a new assembly. A number of congregations,
including a group in Kent, proffered advice, which played some part in the
choice of members in the Barebones Parliament.*

A voluntary meeting has been occasioned to consider how far we might be
useful to our country, though but in the nomination of these which, we
hope, are qualified to and spirited for government most near your late
public desires . . . to wit men fearing God and hating covetousness; judging
this a season in which the Lord doth especially call for the free contribution
of his people to the work which through so much blood, etc. he hath
wrestled into their hands . . . we hope lawyers, especially in practice (we are
for those that out of conscience have laid it by) nor interested ones against
common good (as impropriators generally are, and wilful rigid Presbyterians) shall never warm a seat in the supreme trust more. We are afraid
this burden will never set fast on many shoulders: a few godly wise ones,
will better discharge and dispatch than great numbers, amongst which will
be dilatory proceedings if no dangerous obstructions. We hope that godly
prudent men, though but of mean estates, will not be forgotten . . . for we
had rather maintain such than entrust this cause with men suffocated and
spent in pomps, pleasures and idleness, biassed with greatness and corrupt
friendships. . . . We hope your Lordship [Cromwell] shall find mercy to
carry you through what remains of this blessed work the healing of the
breaches that tyrants of any name have made upon the thing called true

liberty and birthright; and in restoring the paths, viz. right and impartial administration of justice, etc. to dwell in.

The Kentish Churches to Cromwell, 25 May 1653, printed in [21], pp. 95–6.

DOCUMENT 7 **PARLIAMENT CRITICISES THE PROTECTORATE**

A diarist recorded the main points made by the Protector's critics at the start of the 1654 parliament. After the initial storm calmer counsels worked out a compromise by which some features of the Instrument might be amended without destroying its basic principles.

11 September 1654 ... Much more was said on both sides, as to the conveniences and inconveniences of either government, and it was disputed as if they had been in the schools, where each man had liberty to propose his own Utopia, and to frame commonwealths according to his own fancy ...

At length the more moderate sort on both sides were willing to propound expedients; and, accordingly, it was propounded by them who were for the coordination of a single person, that there might be a check, as they called it, upon the Parliament, as to the legislative power in some few things.
1. To avoid the perpetuity, or some other exorbitances in the supremacy of Parliaments. Therefore, a sole person might be conjoined with it to prevent these.
2. As to the militia, that the Parliament might not have the sole disposing power of that.
3. As to religion, that it might not impose what it pleased in that.

As to all other things, they were contented to leave the legislative power entire to Parliament, so as the executive power might be wholly in one sole person; with such qualifications restrictions and instructions, as it should receive from the Parliament.

Goddard's Diary in [5], I, pp. xxxi–xxxii.

DOCUMENT 8 **TROUBLE WITH PARLIAMENT**

Cromwell, disappointed by the First Protectorate Parliament, dissolved it at the earliest opportunity. In this speech, delivered on 25 January 1655, he recited his complaints, and showed how much the MPs' neglect of the army had angered him.

There is another necessity which you have put upon us, and we have not sought ... and instead of seasonable providing for the army, you have laboured to overthrow the government, and the army is now upon free quarter;* and you would never so much as let me hear a tittle from you concerning it. Where is the fault? Has it not been as if you had had a purpose to put this extremity upon us and the nation? I hope this was not in your minds; I am not willing to judge so, but this is the state unto which we are reduced. By the designs of some in the Army, who are now in custody, it was designed to get as many of them as they could, through discontent for want of money, the army being in a barren country near thirty weeks behind in pay, and upon other specious pretences, to march for England out of Scotland, and in discontent to seize their general there . . . that so another might head the army and all this opportunity taken from your delays . . . What could it signify but that the army are in discontent already, and we'll make them live upon stones, we'll make them cast off their governors and discipline?

Writings and Speeches [1], III, p. 593.

DOCUMENT 9   **REPUBLICANS ATTACK THE CONSTITUTION**

The Commonwealthmen consistently opposed the Protectorate and the limited powers accorded to parliament under it. After the experience of the first Protectorate Parliament, Commonwealthmen constantly harried Cromwell, as the following extract shows.

[Parliament] is understood to be a creature of your [Cromwell's] will and power, the definition of the places, the qualification of the persons, the summons, and all other incidents belonging unto it, deriving themselves wholly from you, and your assumed office, so that if there be a flaw in the justice or legality of that which is the foundation [the Instrument] what can be hoped for in the superstructure? . . . Another thing which renders the whole scrupulous is that your Highness should think the people fit to have a share in government and give laws, and yet should make yourself so far paramount to them at the same time as to confine them by instrument and indentures what power they shall delegate to their trustees. If the original of all just power be in the people, as we have been taught by the Parliament, how comes there to be a jurisdiction superior to theirs, which must command them what to do with that power, and what instructions to give those who represent them?

R.G., *A Copy of a Letter from an Officer in the Army in Ireland to his Highness the Lord Protector concerning his changing of the Government* (London, 1656), p. 9.

DOCUMENT 10 A MAJOR-GENERAL AT WORK

The major-generals were at first surprised by the compliance which greeted them, though some suspected its true meaning. The suggestion made here by Major-General Whalley, that the major-generals be added to the commission of the peace, was soon adopted, and as a result their civilian work then eclipsed their military functions.

I am now returned from Lincoln to Nottingham, where yesterday we had a great appearance of the cavaliers, being formerly summoned by us to bring in particulars of their estates, real and personal. Our business goes now very well; and I hope we shall give to you a good account of it. Myself severally . . . writ to you . . . to desire you to send us more of the printed instructions as also some more of your last declarations, as very necessary; but having not heard from you, I renew the request; and likewise that the major-generals may be constituted justices of the peace in the several and particular counties and corporations given them in their charge; for I find it very needful. I was forced at Lincoln, for the composing a long and hot difference there betwixt the major, aldermen and citizens to assume a little more power than (I think) belonged to me . . . I hope after I have gone through all the counties and shall have opportunity to make longer stay in Lincoln and Nottinghamshire, to present you with the names of some gentlemen, that may be fit to be put in the commission of the peace, there being yet scarce enough to carry on the public service.

Major-General Edward Whalley to Secretary Thurloe, Leicester, 24 November 1655, printed in *Thurloe State Papers* [25], IV, p. 197.

DOCUMENT 11 AN AMBIGUOUS RESPONSE TO THE MAJOR-GENERALS

Baxter, the Puritan minister from Kidderminster, succinctly characterised the local major-general.

About this time Cromwell set up his major-generals, and the decimation on the estates of the royalists, called delinquents to maintain them; and James Berry was made major-general of Worcestershire, Shropshire, Herefordshire and North Wales, the countries in which he had formerly lived as a servant (a clerk of iron-works). His reign was modest and short; but hated and scorned by the gentry that had known his inferiority, so that it had been better for him to have chosen a stranger place. And yet many of them attended to him as submissively as if they had honoured him, so significant a thing is power and prosperity to worldly minds.

Reliquiae Baxterianae [3], pp. 97–8.

DOCUMENT 12   A PLAN OF MORAL REFORM

The godly pressed Cromwell to hasten moral reform, and were encouraged by his apparent support of their programme in 1653 and 1655–6. Part of an unusually detailed scheme, by a lawyer, follows:

Grievance . . . that there is no law against lascivious gestures, wanton and filthy dalliance and familiarity, whorish attire, strange fashions, such as are naked breasts, bare shoulders, powdering, spotting, painting the face, curling and shearing of the hair, excess of apparel in servants and mean people. It is offered to consideration: 1. That the justices of the peace at their Quarter-Sessions may bind any such to the good behaviour. 2. That for a whorish attire, something of note be written upon the door of her house to her disgrace, there to continue till she wear sober attire.

It is objected, that there is no certain and clear law to punish profane jesting, fiddling, rhyming, piping, juggling, fortune-telling, tumbling, dancing upon the rope, vaunting, ballad-singing, sword playing, or playing of prizes, ape-carrying, puppet-playing, bear-baiting, bull-baiting, horse-racing, cock-fighting, carding, dicing and other gaming, especially the spending of much time and the adventuring of great sums of money herein. It is offered to consideration: That to the laws already made, 1. that it be in the power of any two justices of the peace to bind to the good behaviour such as are offensive herein; 2. that they be, so long as they use it, uncapable of bearing any office in the Commonwealth; 3. that all payments to the Commonwealth be doubled on such persons.

William Sheppard, *Englands Balme* (London, 1657), pp. 162–3.

DOCUMENT 13   THE DECIMATION ON TAX DEFENDED
                AND ATTACKED

Desborough asked parliament on 25 December 1656 to continue the decimation tax on the royalists, and thereby provoked a fierce debate which ended with the removal of the tax and of the major-generals supported by it. Desborough and Lambert both defended the system; Sir John Hobart and John Trevor were among the numerous country gentlemen who spoke against it.

Desborough. I have a short bill to offer you, for continuance of a tax upon some people, for the maintenance of the militia. It will be for the security of your peace. It can fall upon no persons so fitly as those that occasion the charge. Let us lay the saddle on the right horse. Your friends and enemies have hitherto borne an equal share. There ought to be discrimination; for if your enemies should have prevailed, they would have freed themselves.

Sir John Hobart. If I had been satisfied that this tax might be laid without a breach of your faith, I should not have risen . . . I would have the question plainly put, whether the Act of Oblivion be taken away. Let us have a prospect as well to the honour of a Parliament and the Liberty of Englishmen, as to the safety of the nation. I have an equal respect to all, but let us do things that are just and honest. Must we confirm all that passed, or continue the tax upon them without examining the merits . . .?

Lambert. I am as guilty of the Act of Oblivion as any man. I have laboured to oblige that party; to win them, as much as may be; but find it impossible till time wear out the memory. They are as careful to breed upon their children in the memory of the quarrel as can be. They are, haply, now merry over their Christmas pies, drinking the King of Scots' health or your confusion . . .

Trevor . . . I am not ashamed to plead for my enemies, where justice and the faith of the nation plead for them. What do we by this, but incorporate them against us, and put such a character of distinction upon them, but they will never be reconciled. We do but harden and strengthen them against us, and oblige them to a perpetual enmity. You provoke and unite your enemies and divide yourselves, and necessitate new arms and charges and raise new dangers. You provoke them, by taking away a tenth part from them, and leave them the nine parts to be revenged. I like not this middle way of policy, neither to oblige nor destroy. It leaves things doubtful, and puts men into a constant danger to be undone. To forgive our enemies is God's rule, and it is the only way to make them our friends.

Another argument to me, against this bill, not spoken of, is the consequences of it: a new militia, raised with a tendency to divide this Commonwealth into provinces; a power too great to be bound within any law; in plain terms, to cantonize the nation and prostitute our laws and civil peace, to a power that never was set up in any nation without dangerous consequences. From the time of Charles VII of France, the date of their slaveries began. They expelled their enemies, but since that time, no old laws, no Parliaments, have been which they had as free as any people before. I have discharged my conscience in telling you how much I dread the consequence of it. I am against giving this bill another reading.

Burton [5], I, pp. 230, 240, 315.

DOCUMENT 14   KINGSHIP PROPOSED AND REJECTED

A series of letters from Irish MPs in the 1656–7 parliament kept Henry Cromwell well-informed about the progress of the Humble Petition and Advice. The first letter described the introduction of the scheme; the second the Protector's objections to it, which were never overcome.

(a) Sir Christopher Packe offered this paper to the House . . . Many arraigned him, but upon the question whether it should be read or not the house divided: 144 were for it, 54 against it. This day we contended hard about the manner of considering the paper, and resolved tomorrow morning to read it by parts. Lord Lambert is violently against it. Desborough, Sydenham, Lord Deputy [Fleetwood], Strickland, Pickering and some others of the Council are against it. Lord President Lawrence, Philip Jones, Montagu, Sir Charles Wolseley, Lord Fiennes, Skippon, Thurloe are highly for it. Sir Richard Onslow is head of the country party for it. Sir William Strickland against it. All the long robe [the lawyers] are keenly for it. The Irish all for it but Cooper, Hewson and Sankey. All the Yorkshiremen are against it but Charles Howard.

Anthony Morgan to H. Cromwell, London, 24 February 1656[7], British Library, Lansdowne Ms. 821, f. 294, quoted in Firth [150 *p. 55*].

(b) 3 April 1657: A committee was appointed for a free conference with his Highness to satisfy him of the reason and necessity of their demands, and they have several times attended his Highness upon that occasion, laid down their reasons, and yesterday his Highness gave answer to them, which was to this effect. That for his part he values not one name more than another, that he had rather have any name from this Parliament than any name without it, so much doth he value the authority of Parliament. But in respect many godly men that have hazarded their lives in this cause are dissatisfied with it, and Providence having with the old family eradicated the old title, he thinks it his duty to beg of the Parliament not to put that upon those good men which they cannot swallow, though it may be their weakness. But though men are divided in judgments what his Highness will resolve upon, yet it seems to me that since he allows an indifferency in the thing his great reason will not permit him to balance the resolves of Parliament made upon so great a debate and consideration, with the humour of persons without, that can give little of reason besides this, that godly men are dissatisfied. I believe his Highness is jealous there may be some distemper in the army.

John Bridges to H. Cromwell, London, 13 April 1657, British Library, Lansdowne Ms. 823, f. 27, quoted in Firth [150 *p. 70*].

DOCUMENT 15   **CROMWELL REVIEWS RECENT EVENTS, 1657**

A contemporary account of Cromwell's speech on 7 March 1657 to one hundred army officers in which he set out his thoughts on the Humble Petition and Advice.

I suppose you have heard of the address made by one hundred Officers, to his Highness [Cromwell], yesterday sevennight, that his Highness would not hearken to the title [of King] because it was not pleasing to his army, and was matter of scandal to the people of God, of great rejoicing to the enemy; that it was hazardous to his own person, and of great danger to the three nations; such an assumption making way for Charles Stuart to come in again.

His Highness returned answer presently to this effect: . . . that, for his part, he had never been at any cabal about the same, (hinting by that, the frequent cabals that were against Kingship by certain officers). He said, the time was, when they boggled not at the word [King], for the Instrument by which the Government now stands, was presented to his Highness with the title [King] in it, as some there present could witness, pointing at a principal officer, then in his eye, and he refused to accept of the title. But how it comes to pass that they now startle at that title, they best knew. That, for his part, he loved the title, a feather in a hat, as little as they did. That they had made him their drudge, upon all occasions; to dissolve the Long Parliament, who had contracted evil enough by long sitting; to call a Parliament, or Convention, of their naming [Barebones], who met; and what did they? fly at liberty and property, insomuch as if one man had twelve cows, they held another that wanted cows ought to take share with his neighbour. Who could have said any thing was their own, if they had gone on? After their dissolution, how was I pressed by you . . . for the rooting out of the ministry; nay, rather than fail, to starve them out.

A Parliament was afterwards called [in September 1654]; they sat five months; it is true we hardly heard of them all that time. They took the Instrument into debate, and they must needs be dissolved; and yet stood not the Instrument in need of mending? was not the case hard with me, to be put upon to swear that which was so hard to be kept?

Sometime after that, you thought it was necessary to have Major-Generals; and the first rise to that motion (then was the late general insurrections) was justifiable; and you, Major-Generals, did your parts well. You might have gone on. Who bid you go to the House with a Bill, and there receive a foil?

After you had exercised this power a while, impatient were you till a Parliament was called. I gave my vote against it; but you were confident, by your own strength and interest, to get men chosen to your heart's desire. How have you failed therein, and how much the country hath been disobliged is well known.

That it is time to come to a settlement, and lay aside arbitrary proceedings, so unacceptable to the nation. And by the proceedings of this Parliament, you see they stand in need of a check, or balancing power, (meaning the House of Lords, or a House so constituted) for the case of James Nayler might happen to be your own case. By their judicial power they fall upon life and member, and doth the Instrument enable me to control it?

Burton [5], I, pp. 382–4.

DOCUMENT 16 CROMWELL IS BEGGED TO ADHERE TO
'THE GOOD OLD CAUSE'

Typical of the sentimental appeals which reached Cromwell as he considered whether or not to become king was that of William Bradford, an old soldier and sectary.

I perceive there are a number in Parliament that have voted Kingship for you. I likewise perceive that there is a number there (though the less) that voted against it, and that the greatest part of the officers of the army now near you are against it. I beg and beseech your Highness, nay again and again, with tears and prayers I beseech you to consider what you are doing, after so many declarations and engagements, willingly taken by your direction, by most of the people now subject to you, and after an instrument signed and sworn to by yourself. Consider, my Lord ... and weigh between those two parties voting and dissatisfied. Those that are for a crown, I fear you have little experience of them; the other, most of them, have attended your greatest hazards. The divisions amongst us are like to make us unhappy, unless the Lord prevent it; a divided kingdom cannot stand. ... The Anabaptists say you are a perfidious person, and that because you promised them at a certain day to take away tithes, but did not perform with them ... I am of that number, my Lord, that still loves you, and greatly desires to do so, I having gone along with you from Edge Hill to Dunbar. The experiences you have had of the power of God at these two places, and betwixt them, methinks, should often make you shrink, and be at a stand in this thwarting, threatening change.

William Bradford to Cromwell, 4 March 1657, printed in *State Papers addressed to Cromwell* [21], pp. 141–2.

DOCUMENT 17 A POPULAR FRONT AGAINST THE
PROTECTORATE

The Commonwealthmen, after various unsuccessful attempts, made a tactical alliance in 1658 with discontented sectaries, urban radicals and soldiers. Their demands were embodied in a petition, but Cromwell dissolved parliament before it could be presented. This alliance would bring down Richard Cromwell in May 1659.

Your petitioners humbly pray:
That together with the constant succession of free Parliaments duly chosen, the supreme power and trust which the people (the original of all just power) commit unto them, to make laws, constitutions and officers for the government of the whole, and to call all officers of justice and ministers of

state whatsoever to account, may be so clearly declared and secured against all attempts to the contrary that no question may henceforth arise concerning the same.

That the militia may be settled with such wisdom and full security that it may not be in the power of any to make use thereof against the people, or the successive Parliaments, either to destroy their being or their freedom.

That no money may be levied upon the people (on any pretence whatsoever) but by their common consent in Parliament . . .

And that as the safety of our religion is concerned in the defence of our civil rights, so such provision may now be made for the encouragement of the sincere professors of the same, that no tender conscience may be oppressed . . .

E. H. *A True Copy of a Petition . . . intended to have been delivered to the late Parliament* (London, 1657 [8]), p. 4.

DOCUMENT 18   **CROMWELL AND EUROPE**

A series of works published after 1660 besmirched Cromwell's reputation, and decried the achievements of the Rump. Here Cromwell's record in foreign affairs is contrasted unfavourably with that of the Rump.

The nation being in this flourishing and formidable posture [under the Rump], Cromwell began his usurpation, upon the greatest advantages imaginable, having it in his power to have made peace and profitable leagues, in what manner he pleased with all our neighbours, every one courting us then, and being ambitious of the friendship of England. But as if the Lord had infatuated and deprived him of common sense and reason, he neglected all our golden opportunities, misimproved the victory God had given us over the United Netherlands, making peace (without ever striking a stroke) as soon as ever things came into his hands upon equal terms with them. And immediately after, contrary to our interest, made an unjust war with Spain, and an impolitic league with France, bringing the first thereby under, and making the latter too great for Christendom; and by that means, broke the balance betwixt the two crowns of Spain and France which his predecessors, the Long Parliament, had always wisely preserved.

Bethel [4], p. 3.

GLOSSARY

Anabaptists A religious group which opposed infant baptism, and instead practised adult baptism, insisting that this act was the prerequisite for church membership. The term was more loosely used to associate English Baptists with a sixteenth-century German sect which had been involved in revolt and social protest.

Arminianism The name properly applied to the followers of the Dutch theologian, Arminius, whose views enjoyed popularity in England in the 1620s and 1630s. The doctrine was associated with Archbishop Laud and his allies, and had among its characteristics a stress on man's free will, a rejection of predestination, and a greater stress on the sacraments at the expense of preaching.

Calvinists Properly the followers of the sixteenth-century French theologian, John Calvin. Also applied more loosely in seventeenth-century England to those who accepted Calvin's characteristic beliefs, most notably in predestination, i.e. that God had foreordained who should be saved and who should be damned, and to those who opposed the spread of Arminian ideas of free will after the 1620s.

Commission of the peace A commission issued by the central government to leading gentlemen in each shire. Those so commissioned, the JPs, were empowered to enforce a wide range of laws at the quarter sessions and petty sessions, and also performed other administrative and legal duties in less formal meetings. A place in the commission, though onerous and not salaried, was nevertheless eagerly competed for, both for the authority it bestowed and also as a visible sign of good standing with the government.

Covenanters A name loosely applied to Charles I's opponents in Scotland. Properly it designated those who had signed the National Covenant of 1638, but could also be applied to those who took the Solemn League and Covenant after 1643.

Fifth Monarchists A sect which wanted to bring in the predicted Fifth Monarchy, by the early 1650s thought to be imminent. During the Fifth Monarchy Christ would reign on earth with the Saints for 1,000 years.

Free Quarter A system by which troops, short of pay and supplies, took what they needed from civilians. In theory tickets would be given to the civilians so that they might later be repaid.

Independents The name applied to the Congregationalists who proliferated in the 1640s. They believed that each congregation should be free to worship as it chose.

Justices of the peace (JPs) The name of those nominated in the commission of the peace (see above) to govern each county.

Laudians The followers of Archbishop Laud in the 1630s who were alleged to be exponents of Arminianism (see above) and who were disliked for their emphasis on ceremonial and on their own priestly status.

Militia The traditional defence force in each county, raised, organized and used on a local basis. Its commanders were local gentlemen, named by the central government, who often helped to supply and pay the forces.

Millenarians Those who believed in the coming millennium, the 1,000 years during which Christ and the saints would reign on earth. They included the Fifth Monarchists (see above), but also others less precise about when the millennium would start and less insistent that all should be made ready for the event.

Presbyterians A sect, strong in Scotland since the Reformation and by the 1640s well represented in London and among the clergy, which contended that a Church governed by bishops was contrary to God's word. Presbyterians wished to retain an exclusive and intolerant national Church, organised in parishes and paid by tithes. There was disagreement whether at the highest levels of the structure discipline should be imposed by the clergy alone or by the laity.

Quakers A sect, led by Fox, which made headway after 1652. Its members, like those of other sects, preferred to follow the promptings of the Holy Spirit working within them rather than the teachings of ordained ministers. This led them to tremble or quake, to disturb services, to withhold tithes and to refuse to take oaths.

Ranters A small group which attracted disproportionate attention in the early 1650s. Its members believed that they were chosen by God and could do no wrong. They denied the authority of Scripture, the creeds and the need for ordained ministers, and followed the impulses of the divine spirit working within them.

Saints Those who regarded themselves as the predestined saved and sometimes as having a duty to separate themselves from the unregenerate multitude in the parish church by forming distinct congregations. Some Saints also felt obliged to exercise a godly dictatorship to guarantee or hasten religious reform. The term was often applied promiscuously to separatists or sectaries.

Sectaries A name loosely applied to the members of religious sects, especially to those which opposed an exclusive national Church.

Seekers A group which shared some of the Quakers' characteristics, and, in addition, argued that no true Church existed and that they must wait until God in his own good time sent prophets to establish a new church. The Seekers opposed those sects which wished to hasten that process.

Tithes The payments made by parishioners to support their ministers. Originally they were intended to be one tenth of each parishioner's income or produce, but payment, either in part or in full, was increasingly hard to enforce, especially in towns, and attended by unseemly quarrels. In many cases the money had to be paid to laymen (impropriators) who then allowed the officiating minister a pittance.

BIBLIOGRAPHY

ABBREVIATIONS

EcHR	*Economic History Review*
EHR	*English Historical Review*
HJ	*Historical Journal*
HLQ	*Huntington Library Quarterly*
JBS	*Journal of British Studies*
JEH	*Journal of Ecclesiastical History*
JMH	*Journal of Modern History*
NH	*Northern History*
P&P	*Past and Present*
SCH	*Studies in Church History*
TRHS	*Transactions of the Royal Historical Society*
WHR	*Welsh History Review*

SOURCES

1 Abbott, W.C., *Writings and Speeches of Oliver Cromwell,* 4 vols, Harvard University Press, 1937–47, reprinted Oxford University Press, 1988.

2 Aylmer, G.E. (ed.), *The Levellers and the English Revolution,* Thames & Hudson, 1975.

3 Baxter, Richard, *Reliquiae Baxterianae,* London, 1696, reprinted Dent, 1974.

4 Bethel, Slingsby, *The Worlds Mistake in Oliver Cromwell,* London, 1668, reprinted by *The Rota,* Exeter, 1972.

5 Burton, Thomas, *Diary of Thomas Burton,* (ed.) J.T. Rutt, 4 vols, London 1828, reprinted by Johnson Reprint Company, 1974.

6 Clarendon, Edward Hyde, first Earl of, *History of the Rebellion,* (ed.) W.D. Macray, 6 vols, Oxford, 1888.

7 Cliffe, J.T. (ed.), 'The Cromwellian Decimation Tax of 1655: the Assessment Lists', *Camden Miscellany,* xxxiii, Camden Society, 1996.

8 Dunlop, R.T., *Ireland under the Commonwealth,* 2 vols, Manchester University Press, 1913.

9 Firth, C.H. (ed.), *Clarke Papers,* 4 vols, Camden Society, 1891–1901.

10 Firth, C.H. (ed.), 'Letters concerning the dissolution of Cromwell's last Parliament, 1658,' *EHR,* viii, (1892).

11   Firth, C.H. (ed.), *Nicholas Papers*, 4 vols, Camden Society,
     1886–1920.
12   Firth, C.H. (ed.), *Scotland and the Commonwealth*, Scottish History
     Society, Edinburgh, 1895.
13   Firth C.H. (ed.), *Scotland and the Protectorate*, Scottish History
     Society, Edinburgh, 1899.
14   Firth, C.H. and Rait, R.S. (eds.), *Acts and Ordinances of the
     Interregnum,* 3 vols, London, 1911.
15   Gardiner, S.R., *Constitutional Documents of the Puritan Revolution,*
     Oxford University Press, 1906.
16   Haller, W. (ed.), *Tracts on Liberty in the Puritan Revolution*, 3 vols,
     Columbia University Press, 1934.
17   Harrington, J., *The Political Works*, (ed.) J.G.A. Pocock, Cambridge
     University Press, 1977.
18   Ludlow, E., *Memoirs,* (ed.) C.H. Firth, 2 vols, Oxford, 1894.
19   Macfarlane, A. (ed.), *The Diary of Ralph Josselin, 1616–1683*, British
     Academy, Oxford University Press, 1976.
20   Morton, A.L., *Freedom in Arms*, Lawrence & Wishart, 1975.
21   Nickolls, J. (ed.), *Original Letters and Papers of State ... addressed to
     Oliver Cromwell,* London, 1743.
22   Roberts, M. (ed.), *Swedish Diplomats at Cromwell's Court,
     1655–1656,* Camden Society, 1988.
23   *Somers Tracts* (ed.), W. Scott, 13 vols, London, 1809.
24   Spalding, R. (ed.), *The Diary of Bulstrode Whitelocke, 1605–1675,*
     British Academy, Oxford University Press, 1990.
25   *Thurloe State Papers,* ed. T. Birch, 7 vols, London, 1742.
26   Whitelocke, B., *Memorials of English Affairs*, 4 vols, Oxford 1853.
27   Winstanley, G., *The Law of Freedom and other writings*, (ed.) C. Hill,
     Penguin Books, 1973.
28   Wolfe, D.M., *Leveller Manifestoes of the Puritan Revolution*, Nelson,
     1944.
29   Woodhouse, A.S.P. (ed.), *Puritanism and Liberty*, Dent, 1938.

SECONDARY WORKS: BOOKS

30   Ashley, M.P., *Financial and Commercial Policy of the Commonwealth
     and Protectorate,* Oxford University Press, 1934, reprinted by Cass,
     1962.
31   Aylmer, G.E. (ed.), *The Interregnum: The Quest for Settlement,*
     Macmillan, 1972.
32   Aylmer, G.E., *Rebellion or Revolution? England 1640–1660*, Oxford
     University Press, 1986.
33   Aylmer, G.E., *The State's Servants*, Routledge, 1973.
34   Barnard, T.C., *Cromwellian Ireland*, Oxford University Press, 1975.
35   Blackwood, B.G., *The Lancashire Gentry and the Great Rebellion,*
     Chetham Society, Manchester, 1978.

36 Bottigheimer, K.S., *English Money and Irish Land*, Oxford University Press, 1970.
37 Braddick, M.J., *The Nerves of the State: Taxation and the Financing of the English State, 1558–1714*, Manchester University Press, 1996.
38 Brailsford, H., *The Levellers and the English Revolution*, Cresset Press, 1961, reprinted by Spokesman Books, 1976.
39 Brown, K., *Kingdom or Province? Scotland and the Regal Union, 1603–1715*, Macmillan, 1992.
40 Capp, B.S., *Cromwell's Navy: the Fleet and the English Revolution 1648–1660*, Oxford University Press, 1989.
41 Capp, B.S., *The Fifth Monarchy Men*, Faber, 1972.
42 Coate, Mary, *Cornwall in the Great Civil War and Interregnum*, Oxford University Press, 1933, reprinted by D. Bradford Barton, Truro, 1963.
43 Coleby, A., *Central Government and the Localities: Hampshire 1649–1689*, Cambridge University Press, 1987.
44 Coward, B., *Oliver Cromwell*, Longman, 1991.
45 Cromartie, A., *Sir Matthew Hale, 1609–1676*, Cambridge University Press, 1995.
46 Davis, J.C., *Fear, Myth and History: The Ranters and the Historians*, Cambridge University Press, 1986.
47 Davis, J.C., *Utopia and the Ideal Society*, Cambridge University Press, 1981.
48 Dodd, A.H., *Studies in Stuart Wales*, University of Wales Press, 1952.
49 Dow, Frances, *Cromwellian Scotland*, John Donald, 1979.
50 Everitt, A.M., *The Community of Kent and the Great Rebellion*, Leicester University Press, 1966.
51 Fink, Z.S., *The Classical Republicans*, Evanston University Press, 1945.
52 Firth, C.H., *Cromwell's Army*, Methuen, 1902.
53 Firth, C.H., *The Last Years of the Protectorate*, 2 vols, Longmans, Green & Co., 1909.
54 Firth, C.H., *Oliver Cromwell and the Rule of the Puritans*, London, 1901.
55 Fletcher, A., *A County Community in Peace and War: Sussex 1600–1660*, Longman, 1975.
56 Fletcher, A., *Reform in the Provinces: The Government of Stuart England*, Yale University Press, 1986.
57 Frank, J., *The Levellers*, Harvard University Press, 1955.
58 Gardiner, S.R., *History of the Commonwealth and Protectorate*, 4 vols, Longmans, Green & Co., 1903.
59 Gentles, I., *The New Model Army in England, Ireland and Scotland, 1645–1653*, Blackwell, 1992.
60 Haller, W., *Liberty and Reformation in the Puritan Revolution*, Columbia University Press, 1955.
61 Hardacre, P., *The Royalists during the Puritan Revolution*, Nijhoff, The Hague, 1956.

62   Hill, Christopher, *Change and Continuity in Seventeenth-Century England*, Weidenfeld, 1974.

63   Hill, Christopher, *God's Englishman*, Weidenfeld, 1970.

64   Hill, Christopher, *Puritanism and Revolution*, Secker, 1958.

65   Hill, Christopher, *The World Turned Upside Down*, Temple Smith, 1972.

66   Hinton, R.W.K., *The Eastland Company and the Commonwealth*, Cambridge University Press, 1959.

67   Holmes, C., *Seventeenth-Century Lincolnshire*, Society for Lincolnshire History and Archaeology, 1980.

68   Howell, Roger, *Newcastle-upon-Tyne and the Puritan Revolution*, Oxford University Press, 1967.

69   Hughes, A., *Politics, Society and Civil War in Warwickshire, 1620–1660*, Cambridge University Press, 1987.

70   Hutton, R.A., *The British Republic, 1649–1660*, Macmillan, 1990.

71   Hutton, R.A., *Charles II*, Oxford University Press, 1989.

72   Hutton, R.A., *The Restoration, 1658–1667*, Oxford University Press, 1985.

73   James, Margaret, *Social Problems and Policy during the Puritan Revolution*, Routledge, 1930.

74   Jones, C., Newitt, M. and Roberts, S., (eds), *Politics and People in Revolutionary England*, Blackwell, 1986.

75   Kishlansky, M.A., *The Rise of the New Model Army*, Cambridge University Press, 1979.

76   Lamont, W.M., *Godly Rule: Politics and Religion 1603–1660*, Macmillan, 1969.

77   MacCuarta, B., *Ulster 1641: Aspects of a Rising*, Institute of Irish Studies, Belfast, 1993.

78   Manning, B.S., *1649: The Crisis of the English Revolution*, Bookmarks, 1992.

79   Manning, B.S., *The English People and the English Revolution*, Heinemann, 1976.

80   Manning, B.S. (ed.), *Religion, Politics and the English Civil War*, Arnold, 1973.

81   Matthews, N.L., *William Sheppard*, Cambridge University Press, 1984.

82   McGregor, J.F. and Reay, B. (eds), *Radical Religion and the English Revolution*, Oxford University Press, 1984.

83   Morrill, J.S., *Cheshire 1630–1660*, Oxford University Press, 1974.

84   Morrill, J.S., *The Impact of the English Civil War*, Collins and Brown, 1991.

85   Morrill, J.S., *The Nature of the English Revolution*, Longman, 1993.

86   Morrill, J.S. (ed.), *Oliver Cromwell and the English Revolution*, Macmillan, 1990.

87   Morrill, J.S. (ed.), *Reactions to the English Civil War*, Macmillan, 1982.

88   Morrill, J.S., *The Revolt of the Provinces*, Allen & Unwin, 1976.

89 Morrill, J.S., (ed.), *Revolution and Restoration: England in the 1650s*, Collins and Brown, 1992.

90 Morton, A.L., *The World of the Ranters*, Lawrence & Wishart, 1970.

91 Mowl, T. and Earnshaw, B., *Architecture without Kings: The Rise of Puritan Classicism under Cromwell*, Manchester University Press, 1995.

92 Nuttall, G.F., *Richard Baxter*, Nelson, 1965.

93 Nuttall, G.F., *Visible Saints: the Congregational Way 1640–60*, Oxford University Press, 1957.

94 Ohlmeyer, J.H., *Civil War and Restoration in Three Stuart Kingdoms: The Career of Randal MacDonnell, marquis of Antrim, 1609–1683*, Cambridge University Press, 1993.

95 Ohlmeyer, J.H. (ed.), *Ireland from Independence to Occupation 1641–1660*, Cambridge University Press, 1995.

96 Pennington, D.H. and Thomas, K.V., *Puritans and Revolutionaries*, Oxford University Press, 1978.

97 Pincus, S.P.A., *Protestantism and Patriotism: Ideologies and the Making of English Foreign Policy 1650–1668*, Cambridge University Press, 1996.

98 Ramsey, R.W., *Henry Cromwell*, Longmans, Green & Co., 1933.

99 Ramsey, R.W., *Richard Cromwell*, Longmans, Green & Co., 1935.

100 Reay, B., *The Quakers and the English Revolution*, Temple Smith, 1985.

101 Richards, Thomas, *Religious Developments in Wales 1654–1662*, National Eisteddfod Association, London, 1923.

102 Richardson, R.C. (ed.), *Images of Oliver Cromwell*, Manchester University Press, 1993.

103 Richardson, R.C. (ed.), *Town and Countryside in the English Revolution*, Manchester University Press, 1992.

104 Roberts, S.K., *Recovery and Restoration in an English County; Devon Local Administration, 1646–1670*, University of Exeter Press, 1985.

105 Roots, Ivan (ed.), *Cromwell: A Profile*, Macmillan, 1973.

106 Roots, Ivan, *The Great Rebellion*, Batsford, 1966.

107 Scott, J., *Algernon Sidney and the English Republic*, Cambridge University Press, 1988.

108 Shaw, W.A., *A History of the English Church . . . 1640–1660*, 2 vols, Longmans, Green & Co., 1900.

109 Sherwood, Roy, *The Court of Oliver Cromwell*, Croom Helm, 1977.

110 Smith, N., *Literature and Revolution in England, 1640–1660*, Yale University Press, 1994.

111 Spalding, Ruth, *The Improbable Puritan: A Life of Bulstrode Whitelocke*, Faber, 1975.

112 Stevenson, David, *Revolution and Counter-Revolution in Scotland*, Camden Society, 1975.

113 Tolmie, M., *The Triumph of the Saints*, Cambridge University Press, 1977.

114 Trevor-Roper, H.R., *Religion, the Reformation and Social Change,* Macmillan, 1967.
115 Underdown, D., *Pride's Purge,* Oxford University Press, 1971.
116 Underdown, D., *Revel, Riot and Rebellion,* Oxford University Press, 1985.
117 Underdown, D., *Royalist Conspiracy in England,* Yale University Press, 1960.
118 Underdown, D., *Somerset in the Civil War and Interregnum,* David and Charles, 1973.
119 Vann, Richard, *The Social Development of English Quakerism,* Harvard University Press, 1969.
120 Vaughan, Robert, *The Protectorate of Oliver Cromwell,* 2 vols, London, 1838.
121 Veall, Donald, *The Popular Movement for Law Reform 1640–1660,* Oxford University Press, 1970.
122 Venning, T., *Cromwellian Foreign Policy,* Macmillan, 1995.
123 Webster, Charles, *The Great Instauration,* Duckworth, 1975.
124 Wedgwood, C.V., *The Trial of Charles I,* Collins, 1964.
125 Wilson, C.H., *Profit and Power,* Longmans, Green & Co., 1957.
126 Woolrych, A.H., *Commonwealth to Protectorate,* Oxford University Press, 1982.
127 Woolrych, A.H., Introduction to *Complete Prose Works of John Milton, VII, 1659–60,* Columbia University Press, 1974.
128 Woolrych, A.H., *Penruddock's Rising,* Historical Association, 1955.
129 Woolrych, A.H., *Soldiers and Statesmen: the General Council of the Army and its Debates, 1647–1648,* Oxford University Press, 1987.
130 Worden, Blair, *The Rump Parliament,* Cambridge University Press, 1974.

SECONDARY WORKS: ARTICLES AND ESSAYS

131 Aylmer, G.E., 'Who was ruling in Herefordshire from 1645–1661?' *Transactions of the Woolhope Naturalists' Field Club,* x, 1972.
132 Aylmer, G.E., 'Did the Ranters Exist?', *P&P,* cxvii 1987.
133 Barnard, T.C., 'Crises of Identity among Irish Protestants, 1641–1685', *P&P,* cxxvii, 1990.
134 Barnard, T.C., 'Land and the Limits of Loyalty: the 2nd Earl of Cork and 1st Earl of Burlington (1612–1698)', in Barnard, T. and Clark, J. (eds), *Lord Burlington: Architecture, Art and Life,* Hambledon Press, 1995.
135 Barnard, T.C., 'Planters and policies in Cromwellian Ireland', *P&P,* lxi, 1973.
136 Barnard, T.C., 'Scotland and Ireland in the Later Stewart Monarchy', in Ellis, S.G. and Barber, S. (eds), *Conquest and Union: Fashioning a British State 1485–1725,* Longman, 1995.

137 Beier, A.L. 'Poor relief in Warwickshire, 1630–60', *P&P*, xxxv, 1966.
138 Brenner, R., 'The civil war politics of London's merchant community', *P&P*, lviii, 1973.
139 Carlin, N. 'Extreme or Mainstream? The English Independents and the Cromwellian Reconquest of Ireland, 1649–51', in Bradshaw, B., Hadfield, A. and Maley, W. (eds), *Representing Ireland*, Cambridge University Press, 1993.
140 Carlin, N. 'The Levellers and the conquest of Ireland', *HJ*, xxx, 1987.
141 Catterall, R.H.C., 'The failure of the humble petition and advice', *American Historical Review*, ix, 1903.
142 Cole, A., 'Quakers and the English Revolution', *P&P*, x, 1956, reprinted in *Crisis in Europe 1550–1660* (ed.), T. Aston, Routledge, 1965.
143 Cotterell, M., 'Interregnum law reform: the Hale Commission of 1652', *EHR*, lxxxiii, 1968.
144 Crawford, P., 'Charles Stuart, "that man of blood"', *JBS*, xvi, 1977.
145 Davis, J.C., 'Fear, Myth and Furore: Reappraising the Ranters', *P&P*, cxxix, 1990.
146 Davis, J.C., 'The Levellers and Democracy', *P&P*, xl, 1968.
147 Durston, C., ' "Unhallowed Wedlocks": The Regulation of Marriage during the English Revolution', *HJ*, xxxi, 1988.
148 Durston, C., 'Puritan Rule and the Failure of Cultural Revolution, 1645–1660', in Durston, C. and Eales, J. (eds), *The Culture of English Puritanism, 1560–1700*, Macmillan, 1996.
149 Farnell, J.E., 'The Navigation Act of 1651', *EcHR*, 2nd series, xvi, 1963–4.
150 Firth, C.H., 'Cromwell and the Crown', *EHR*, xvii (1902) and xviii, 1903.
151 Firth, C.H., 'Cromwell and the expulsion of the Long Parliament in 1653', *EHR*, viii, 1893.
152 Firth, C.H., 'Cromwell and the insurrection of 1655', *EHR*, iii, 1888.
153 Firth, C.H., 'The expulsion of the Long Parliament', *History*, ii, 1917–18.
154 Forster, G.C.F., 'County government in Yorkshire during the Interregnum', *NH*, xii, 1976.
155 Gaunt, P., ' "The Single Person's Confidants and Dependants"? Oliver Cromwell and his Protectoral Councillors', *HJ*, xxxii, 1989.
156 Gaunt, P., 'Cromwell's Purge? Exclusions and the first Protectorate Parliament', *Parliamentary History*, vi, 1987.
157 Gentles, I., 'The sales of the crown lands during the English Revolution', *EcHR*, 2nd series, xxvi, 1973.
158 Groenveld, S., 'The English Civil Wars as a Cause of the First Anglo-Dutch War, 1640–52', *HJ*, xxx, 1987.
159 Habbakuk, H.J., 'The land settlement and the restoration of Charles II', *TRHS*, 5th series, xxviii, 1978.

160 Habbakuk, H.J., 'Landowners and the Civil War', *EcHR*, 2nd series, xviii, 1965.

161 Habbakuk, H.J., 'Public finance and the sale of confiscated property during the Interregnum', *EcHR*, 2nd series, xv, 1962–3.

162 Hardacre, P., 'William Boteler: a Cromwellian oligarch', *HLQ*, xi, 1947.

163 Heath, G.D., 'Making the Instrument of Government', *JBS*, vi, 1967, reprinted in Roots [105].

164 Henderson, B.L.K., 'The Commonwealth Charters', *TRHS*, 3rd series, vi, 1912.

165 Hirst, D., 'The Failure of Godly Rule in the English Republic', *P&P*, cxxxii, 1991.

166 Holiday, P.G., 'Land sales and repurchases in Yorkshire after the Civil Wars', *NH*, v, 1970.

167 Hughes, A., 'The Pulpit Guarded: Confrontations between Orthodox and Radicals in Revolutionary England', in Laurence, A., Owens, W.R. and Sim, S. (eds), *John Bunyan and his England, 1628–1688*, Hambledon Press, 1990.

168 Ingram, M.J., 'Religion, Communities and Moral Discipline in Late-Sixteenth and Early-Seventeenth-Century England', in von Greyerz, K. (ed.), *Religion and Society in Early Modern Europe*, Allen and Unwin, 1984.

169 James, M., 'The political importance of the tithes controversy', *History*, xxvi, 1941–2.

170 Jones, J.G., 'Caernarvonshire administration: the activities of the justices of the peace, 1603–1660', *WHR*, v, 1970–1.

171 Kupperman, K.O., 'Errand to the Indies', *William and Mary Quarterly*, xlv, 1988.

172 Morrill, J.S. and Walter, J.D., 'Order and Disorder in the English Revolution', in Fletcher A. and Stevenson, J. (eds), *Order and Disorder in Early Modern England*, Cambridge University Press, 1985.

173 Pearl, V., 'Oliver St John and the "middle group" in the Long Parliament', *EHR*, lxxx, 1966.

174 Phillips, C.B., 'County committees and local government in Cumberland and Westmorland 1642–1660', *NH*, v, 1970.

175 Phillips, C.B., 'The royalist north: the Cumberland and Westmorland gentry, 1642–1660', *NH*, xiv, 1978.

176 Pinckney, P.J., 'Bradshaw and Cromwell in 1656', *HLQ*, xxx, 1966–7.

177 Pinckney, P.J., 'The Cheshire election of 1656', *Bulletin of the John Rylands Library*, xlix, 1966–7.

178 Pocock, J.G.A., 'James Harrington and "the good old cause"', *JBS*, x, 1970.

179 Prestwich, M., 'Diplomacy and trade in the Protectorate', *JMH*, xxii, 1950.

180 Rannie, D.W., 'Cromwell's major-generals', *EHR*, x, 1895.

181 Reay, B., 'Quaker opposition to tithes 1652–60', *P&P*, lxxxvi, 1980.
182 Roberts, M., 'Cromwell and the Baltic', *EHR*, lxxvi, 1961, reprinted in M. Roberts, *Essays in Swedish History*, Weidenfeld, 1967.
183 Roberts, S.K., 'Fornication and Bastardy in Mid-Seventeenth-Century Devon: How was the Act of 1650 Enforced?', in Rule, J. (ed.), *Outside the Law: Studies in Crime and Order, 1650–1850*, Exeter University Press, 1982.
184 Roots, I., 'Swordsmen and decimators', in R.H. Parry (ed), *The English Civil War and After*, Macmillan, 1970.
185 Roy, I., 'England Turned Germany? The Aftermath of the Civil War in its European Context', *TRHS*, 5th series, xxviii, 1978.
186 Thirsk, J., 'The sales of royalist land during the Interregnum', *EcHR*, 2nd series, v, 1952–3.
187 Underdown, D., 'Cromwell and the officers, February 1658', *EHR*, lxxxiii, 1968.
188 Woolrych, A., 'The calling of Barebone's Parliament', EHR, lxxx, 1965.
189 Woolrych, A., 'The Cromwellian Protectorate: a Military Dictatorship?', *History*, lxxi, 1990.
190 Woolrych, A., ' "The good old cause" and the fall of the Protectorate', *Cambridge HJ*, xiii, 1957.
191 Worden, B., 'The Bill for a new representative: the dissolution of the Long Parliament, April 1653', *EHR*, lxxxvi, 1971.
192 Worden, B., 'Cromwell and the Sin of Achan', in Beales, D. and Best, G.F.A. (eds), *History, Society and the Churches*, Cambridge University Press, 1985.
193 Worden, B., 'English Republicanism', in Burns, J.H. and Goldie, M. (eds), *Cambridge History of Political Thought 1450–1750*, Cambridge University Press, 1991.
194 Worden, B., 'Providence and Politics in Cromwellian England', *P&P*, cix, 1985.
195 Worden, B., 'Toleration and the Cromwellian Protectorate', *SCH*, xxi, 1984.

INDEX

Acts of Parliament: Adultery Act,
   19–20, 26; Blasphemy Act,
   19–20, 26, 58; for church
   attendance, repealed, 17, 19; for
   a New Representative, 22–3; for
   propagating the gospel, 17, 20;
   Navigation Act, 18–19; of
   Oblivion, 51, 58, 89; passed by
   Barebones, 30; Triennial Act, 37,
   60
adultery, 20, 74–5
alehouses, 51, 54–5, 74
Anabaptists, 20, 31, 41, 92, 94
Argyll, marquess of, see Campbell,
   Archibald
Arminianism, 24–5, 94, 95
army, 1–4, 5–7, 8, 9, 11, 12,
   14–20, 28–9, 35, 38, 39, 46,
   50–1, 54, 58–64, 67–8, 70–2,
   74, 75, 78–9, 80, 83, 86, 88–9,
   90–1, 92–3, 95
Ashley Cooper, Anthony, 44, 47,
   59

Baltic, 42–3, 76–7
Baptists, 41, 94
Barebone, Praise-God, 29
Barnstaple, 74
Baxter, Richard, 78, 87
Beake, Robert, 55
Bedford, earl of, see Russell,
   Francis
Bennet, Robert, 13
Berkeley, Sir John, 49
Berry, James, 50, 51, 87
Bethel, Slingsby, 87

Bible, 19, 26, 29, 31, 33
Biddle, John, 46
Birch, John, 44
Birch, Thomas, 13
births, marriages and deaths,
   registering of, 30
bishops and episcopacy, 1, 13, 17,
   18, 19, 20, 38, 41–2, 49, 52, 61,
   68, 75
boroughs, 22, 37, 56, 71, 73, 74,
   75, 87
Boyle, Roger, Lord Broghill, 44,
   46, 59–60, 64, 72
Bradford, William, 92
Bradshaw, John, 44
Bristol, 58, 75
Buckinghamshire, 34

Calvinism, 25–6, 42, 53, 75, 94
Cambridge University, 42
Campbell, Archibald, 1st marquess
   of Argyll, 16
Catholics, 14–15, 20, 25, 30, 37,
   38, 41, 42, 44, 49, 62, 71–2,
   74–5, 76, 82–3
Chancery, 32–3, 34, 40–1, 45, 46
Charles I, 1–4, 5–7, 8, 10, 13–16,
   35, 42–3, 70, 71, 72–3, 77, 81,
   94
Charles II, 8, 14–17, 18, 40, 48–9,
   51, 58, 63, 64, 65, 66, 67–9, 70,
   71, 72, 81, 84–5, 89, 92
Cheshire, 53, 54–5
Chester, 75
Church, 6, 8, 9, 15–16, 17–18,
   19–20, 24, 25, 30–2, 33, 38,

41–2, 46, 53, 57–8, 60–1, 73–5,
  84–5, 94–6
cloth trade, 43
Commission of the Peace, *see*
  justices of the peace
Committee of Safety (1659), 68
Commonwealthmen, 28, 44–6, 56,
  57, 64–5, 67–8, 75–6, 82–3,
  86–7, *see also* republicanism
Confession of faith, 41, 42, 61
Cony, George, 47–8, 63
Cooper, Thomas, 90
Cornwall, 13, 51
Council of State, 11, 28, 30, 35–6,
  38, 45, 47, 50, 53, 60, 63–4, 66,
  90
Covenanters, 16, 94
Coventry, 55, 75
Cromwell, Henry, 40, 59–60, 73,
  90–1
Cromwell, Oliver, 5–7, 9, 12,
  13–17, 20, 22–34, 35–66, 70,
  73, 75, 76–9, 80–2, 83–4,
  85–93
Cromwell, Richard, 67–8
Cunningham, William, 9th earl of
  Glencairn, 40

debtors, 6, 18, 30
decimation tax, 50–1, 54, 58–60,
  87, 88–9
Denmark, 42, 76–7
Desborough, John, 50, 58, 61, 62,
  67, 81, 88, 90
Devon, 34, 50, 75
Diggers, 13
Dorchester, 74
dress, reform of, 88
Drogheda, 15
drunkenness, 26, 51, 52, 54–5, 74
Dublin, 15, 39
Dunbar, battle of, 16, 66, 80, 92
Dunkirk, 76

Edgehill, battle of, 92
education, 19, 76, *see also* schools

elections, 21–2, 27, 43–4, 56, 57,
  64
electoral reform, 6, 8–9, 21–3, 25,
  37, 45–6
Elizabeth, Queen, 53
Engagement, Oath of, 28, 39
English, a chosen people, 15, 26, 27
entertainments, 26, 51–2, 74, 88
episcopacy, *see* bishops
Essex, 50, 74–5
Europe, 3, 8, 14, 43, 76–7, 93, *see*
  also foreign policy

Fairfax, Thomas, 5, 6, 7, 16
Fiennes, Nathaniel, 61, 90
Fiennes, William, 1st Viscount Saye
  and Sele, 64
Fifth Monarchists, 20, 24, 27–8,
  30, 32, 33, 44, 94–5
Fleetwood, Charles, 39, 40, 50, 61,
  62, 67, 90
foreign policy, 18–19, 33, 42–3,
  55–6, 64–5, 76–7, 93
Fox, George, 95
Foxe, John, 26
France, 14, 42, 55–6, 76–7, 89, 93
franchise, 22, 25, 37, 43–4, 45–6

Germany, 76, 94
Glencairn, Lord, *see* Cunningham,
  William
Gloucester, Prince Henry, duke of,
  81–2
Glynn, John, 60, 64
godly rule, 24–34, 35, 50–6, 68,
  72, 74–5, 78–9, 84–5, 88
Goffe, William, 54
'good old cause', 47, 64–5, 92–3

Hale, Matthew, 21, 32, 39
Hampden's Case, 47
Hampton Court, 40, 79
Harrison, Thomas, 20, 24, 28, 29,
  35, 39, 81
Haselrig, Arthur, 44, 56, 64
Henrietta Maria, 49

Herbert, Sir Edward, 49
Herefordshire, 34, 87
Hewson, John, 90
Hickman, William, 82–3
Hispaniola, 43, 63
Hobart, Sir John, 89
Holland, 4, 18–19, 33, 42–3,
    75–7, 94
Howard, Charles, 90
Humble Petition and Advice,
    59–63, 64, 65, 89–93
Hyde, Edward, 48, 63, 68

Independents, 41, 61, 75, 95, *see
    also* sectaries
Instrument of Government, 35–8,
    45–7, 57–9, 62–3, 85–6, 90–1
Ireland, 5, 8, 14–16, 18, 22, 26,
    30, 31, 35, 37, 39, 40, 47, 50,
    59–60, 70, 71–3, 74, 75, 78, 83,
    89–90
Ireton, Henry, 12, 26, 35

Jamaica, 76
James I, 42
James II, formerly duke of York, 81
Jermyn, Henry, 1st Baron, 49
Jews, 29
Jones, Philip, 61, 90
justices of the peace, 1, 2, 19, 25,
    26, 29, 34, 40, 53–5, 65–6, 71,
    74–5, 87–8, 94, 95

Kelsey, Thomas, 54
Kent, 13, 29, 54, 84
kingship, 59–63, 65, 67, 89–93,
    see also monarchy

Lambert, John, 33, 35, 50, 58,
    61–2, 63–4, 67, 89, 90–1
Lancashire, 13, 54
land, ownership and tenure of, 8,
    13, 17, 40, 48, 71–4
Laud, William, 24–5, 26, 94, 95
law courts, 2, 9, 32–4, 39, 47–8,
    74–5

law reform, 6, 9, 15–16, 17, 20–1,
    24, 25, 26, 29, 32–3, 40– 1, 45,
    68, 73, 82–3, 84–5
Lawrence, Henry, 61, 90
lawyers, 21, 28–33, 39, 41, 46,
    47–8, 59, 63, 80–2, 84, 90
Lenthall, William, 80–1
Levellers, 6, 8–9, 11–13, 26, 44,
    48, 62, 64–5
Lewes, 74
Lilburne, John, 12, 39
Lincoln, 87
Livesey, Michael, 13
London, 2, 3, 6, 8, 10, 12–13, 27,
    39, 41, 47, 50, 52, 61, 64, 67,
    68, 75, 77, 95
Lords, House of, 1, 7, 13, 25, 26,
    36, 58, 60, 63, 64, 91
Louis XIV, 77
Ludlow, Edmund, 3, 39, 47

major-generals, 50–6, 57–9, 61,
    87–9, 91
marriage, civil, 30, 74
Marten, Henry, 3, 9
Mediterranean, 43
Middlesex, 75
militia, 38, 39, 50–1, 54, 85, 88–9,
    93, 95
millenarianism, 24, 28–9, 30–1,
    39, 84–5, 95
ministers of state, 1, 60, 68, 92–3
monarchy, 3, 7, 8, 10, 11, 13, 47,
    59–63, 68, 74, 78, 80–3, *see
    also* kingship
Monck, George, 40
Montagu, Edward, 61, 90
Morley, Herbert, 13

Naseby, battle of, 5
navy, 18–19, 23, 38, 61, 70, 78
Nayler, James, 57–8, 91
Norfolk, 50
Norwich, 75
north of England, 9, 17, 20, 26
Nottingham, 87

Onslow, Sir Richard, 60, 64, 90
ordinances, 41, 42, 46, 47, 52–5
Owen, John, 20, 32, 41, 63
Oxfordshire, 50
Oxford University, 42, 43, 79

Packe, Sir Christopher, 89
parishes, 17, 19, 31, 41, 55, 74–5
Parliament, Barebones (1653),
    27–34, 38–9, 44, 52, 84, 91
Parliament, Convention (1660), 68
Parliament, First Protectorate
    (1654–5), 36, 37–8, 41, 43–7,
    49, 85–6, 91
Parliament, Long (1640–8), 1–3, 6,
    8–9, 14–16, 24–6, 28, 40, 44,
    65, 67–9, 76–7, 82, 84
Parliament, Scottish, 17
Parliament, Second Protectorate
    (1656–8), 56, 57–65, 89–91,
    92–4
Parliament, of 1659, 67
Penruddock, John, 49
Penruddock's rising, 48–50
Pickering, Sir Gilbert, 90
poor relief, 6, 19, 26, 27, 30, 51,
    55, 70, 74
Portugal, 43, 76
Presbyterianism, 14, 16–17, 25,
    27–8, 29, 30, 40, 41, 48, 59, 72,
    75, 84, 95
prices, 2, 12, 55, 74
Pride, Thomas, 3, 62
Prideaux, Edmund, 76
Pride's Purge, 3
Privy Council, 11, 26, 36
protector, office of, 35–6, 44, 45,
    85, 86; *see also* Cromwell,
    Oliver; Instrument of Government
Protestantism, endangered, 25, 77;
    promoted, 9, 15, 17, 19, 20,
    24–7, 29, 30–1, 41–3, 52–4, 55,
    74–5, 77–9
Pula Rum, 76
Pym, John, 1, 11, 18, 24, 25, 36,
    47, 60

Pyne, John, 13

Quakers, 57–8, 66, 70, 75, 95, 96

Ranters, 20, 57, 95
reformation of manners, 52, 53,
    54–5, 74–5, 88
religious toleration, 2, 9, 17,
    19–20, 24–5, 38, 41, 46, 57– 8,
    60–1, 73, 75, 91, 93
republicanism, 4, 10, 11, 79, 81–3,
    85, 86, 92–3
royalism and royalists, 13–14, 15,
    16–17, 18, 28, 37, 41, 42, 44,
    47–51, 59–60, 63, 65–6, 72,
    73–4, 79, 80–2, 88–9
Royal Society, 76
Russell, Francis, 4th earl of
    Bedford, 1
Rye, 74

Sabbatarianism, 26, 52, 74
St James's Palace, 40
St John, Oliver, 24, 25, 59, 64, 76,
    81
Salisbury, 49
Sankey, Jerome, 90
Saye and Sele, Lord, *see* Fiennes,
    William
schools and schoolmasters, 41, 76
Scot, Thomas, 44, 64
Scotland, 2, 3, 8, 14, 16, 17, 22,
    26, 37, 40, 47, 59–60, 70, 71–2,
    73, 75, 80, 83–4, 86, 94, 95
Sealed Knot, 49; *see also* royalism
Second Civil War, 3, 6–7, 14, 15,
    16
sectaries, 8, 9, 12, 25, 29, 31–2,
    38, 39, 48, 62, 64, 68, 75, 92, 96
Seekers, 20, 96
Sheppard, William, 88
Shropshire, 87
Skippon, Philip, 90
Somerset, 13, 51
Spain, 14, 42–3, 56, 64, 65, 70,
    77, 93

Staffordshire, 54
Strickland, William, 90
Strickland, Sir William, 90
Suffolk, 29
Surrey, 13, 34
Sussex, 13, 54, 66
Sweden, 43, 76–7
Switzerland, 76
Sydenham, William, 90

Taunton, 75
taxation, 2, 5, 8, 17, 18, 33, 37,
    38, 40, 44, 45, 46–8, 50– 1, 54,
    56, 62, 64, 70–1, 73–4, 75, 77,
    87, 88–9
Thurloe, John, 47, 61, 76, 87, 90
tithes, 19, 31–2, 33, 38, 41, 57,
    68, 95, 96
trade, 6, 8, 12, 19, 43, 73, 74,
    76–7, 83
Treasury, 40
Trevor, Sir John, 89
triers and ejectors, 41, 46, 52
trustees for the maintenance of
    ministers, 42

United Provinces, *see* Holland
universities, 30, 42

vagabonds, 51–2, 55, 74
Venice, 4

wages, 55
Wagstaff, Sir Joseph, 49
Wales, 9, 17, 20, 24, 26, 29, 31,
    50, 61, 65–6, 87
weights and measures, regulated,
    27, 55, 74
Wexford, 15
Whalley, Edward, 81, 87
Whitelocke, Bulstrpde, 59, 60, 64,
    78, 81
Widdrington, Sir Thomas, 81
Wimbledon, 64
Wolseley, Sir Charles, 44, 60, 61,
    64, 90
women, 19, 58, 74–5, 88
Worcester, battle of, 17, 66, 80
Worcestershire, 87
Worsley, Charles, 54–5

Yorkshire,· 34, 90

RELATED TITLES

S J Houston, *James I*
Second Edition (1995)   0 582 20911 0

'Stan Houston's *James I* was first published in 1973 and the degree to which there have been changes, in fact it is very much a new book, reflect how historians' views of England's first Stuart king have been revised. The 1995 James is a far shrewder, abler monarch than the 1973 James.'

Teaching History

Brian Quintrell, *Charles I 1625–1640*
(1993)   0 582 00354 7

'The author is a distinguished historian, whose influential work hitherto has been largely confined to specialist journals. His decision to write for a more general audience is to be welcomed, and undergraduates as well as sixth-formers will find this book a fine introduction to a complex period. ... There is also a good selection of documents, all of them important, and some printed for the first time or rescued from obscurity.'

History Review

Martyn Bennett, *The English Civil War 1640–1649*
(1995)   0 582 35392 0

'Martyn Bennett's study of the English Civil War is a new and much welcomed book examining events between 1640 and 1649. It is one of the best short studies of that confused decade that I have read and takes account of recent research on the "British" and royalist dimensions.'

Teaching History

John Miller, *The Restoration and the England of Charles II*
Second Edition (1997)   0 582 29223 9

This key *Seminar Study* was first published as *Restoration England: The Reign of Charles II* in 1985. Unavailable for several years the book has now been heavily revised, and expanded, to take account of over ten years of new scholarship. In particular, the Second Edition reflects new work done on political parties, the constitution, taxation, the church, and the legacy of the civil wars. Throughout, complex issues of change over time are explained as clearly and as concisely as possible and the Restoration is placed in the wider context of the development of England in the seventeenth century.

John Miller, *The Glorious Revolution*
Second Edition (1997)   0 582 29222 0

First published in 1983, John Miller's *Glorious Revolution* has established itself as the standard, authoritative introduction to this subject. The Second Edition includes a fuller discussion of Scotland and Ireland (where the Revolution was far from bloodless), the growth of the fiscal-military state, and religion and the Revolution. It reflects the new work published, in particular, in the wake of the tercentenary in 1988.

Barry Coward, *Social Change and Continuity: England 1550–1750*
Revised Edition (1997)   0 582 29442 8

This book outlines the major social changes that occurred in England in the two hundred years after the Reformation. The book's main argument is that, momentous as they were, the social changes of the period should not be seen as part of an inevitable development of 'modern society'; instead the book shows that social changes combined with social continuity to produce a distinctive early modern English society. For the Revised Edition the author has made only modest changes to the main text but has thoroughly updated the extensive bibliography.

R J Acheson, *Radical Puritans in England 1550–1660*
(1990)   0 582 35515 X

This study of religious tensions in Early Modern England explores the different religious separatist movements between 1550 and 1660. The author considers why the radical cause changed from being 'no more than an irritation at parochial level' during the reign of James I into 'a united force in a common opposition to episcopacy' during the time of Archbishop Laud, and finally became so fragmented that it could offer no coherent opposition to the restored monarchy in 1660.

Henry Roseveare, *The Financial Revolution 1660–1760*
(1991)   0 582 35449 8

Between 1660 and 1760 Britain changed from being a defeated, humiliated power to one of the recognised "Great Powers" of Europe. Underlying this transformation was her immeasurably stronger financial position by the close of the Seven Years War in 1763. In this innovative *Seminar Study* Professor Roseveare explores the reasons for this "Financial Revolution". He considers not only the obvious financial developments but also the whole complex of social, political, administrative and constitutional developments which transformed the willingness of the British people to finance, by high taxation and loans, the exploits of their parliamentary government.